The Five Crossroads

Unlocking the Secrets to Your Retirement Journey

Eric L. Scott

Copyright © 2012 Eric L. Scott. All rights reserved.
This book is intended to be helpful to retirees and those about to retire by offering valuable financial information. The author and his creative team have done their best to produce the most accurate general information. However, every individual's situation is different. This book is not intended to replace the advice of a financial advisor, accountant or attorney. Please consult a financial advisor or other financial professional before taking action based upon the advice in this book.

Credits:
Writing—
Written by Eric L. Scott
Writing Consultation by Paul Scott
Editing—
Edited by Lola Dunn
Cover Art—
Budi Saputra

ISBN: 0-6156-4631-X
ISBN-13: 9780615646312

dedication: To my wife Sherri,
for her love, support and standing by me
through all my journeys.
.

Table of Contents

About Eric vi
Foreword..viii
Chapter I (The Letter) 1
Chapter II (Tea and Taxes) 13
Chapter III (The Four Pails) 25
Chapter IV (The Three-Legged Stool).............................35
Chapter V (Cornerstone Construction)...........................47
Chapter VI (The Financial House) 61
Chapter VII (Staying Afloat) 75
Chapter VIII (Leaving a Legacy) 85
Chapter IX (Final Reflections) 99

About Eric
By Paul Scott

Eric L. Scott, my father, is the President and founder of Eric Scott Financial. But he's also much more than that. Eric is first and foremost a husband and a father. He loves spending time with his children (and now grandchildren) and, after 30+ years of marriage, he still gets that loving twinkle in his eye when he looks at my mother.

He has a kind heart. There wasn't a time I remember growing up when my father wasn't doing whatever he could to help those around him. Sometimes it wasn't anything more than stopping by someone's house to say hello but I remember seeing the smiles on their faces when he did. It meant the world to them...and *that* meant the world to him.

Following that same path in life, Eric has been in the financial industry since 1983 and has never looked back. He has loved visiting with people as they've come into his office and enjoys helping them accomplish what they'd only dreamed of during their retirement.

Eric and his team created something special when they designed *The Five Crossroads*. They took the average retirement plan and looked at it from every angle possible. They researched and read, they learned and studied, until they finally developed the all-inclusive Five Crossroads Retirement Plan.

Eric has presented the Five Crossroads and the important and invaluable knowledge within through several of St. George, Utah's avenues:

He hosts a radio program every Monday at 4pm on Fox News 1450 AM, he has appeared on local television channels such as KCSG, and he even teaches financial classes at Dixie State College.

Though this is Eric's first book, it isn't the first book in which he has offered his knowledge. In 2011, he contributed to "Coach Pete" D'Arruda's book *Have You Been Talking to Financial Aliens?* by answering several frequently asked financial and retirement questions.

foreword: My mother and father felt it was important to teach me certain values when I was a young man. They taught me the importance of serving others and the value of a hard day's work.

I carried these values into my adult life, and especially into my career. I made it my goal to help make peoples' lives better than before I met them.

Throughout my career as a retirement guide, I have been striving to preserve that mission and do my best to educate and serve people.

Many people—mentors, clients, family and friends—have encouraged me to write a book. For years, I felt overwhelmed by the idea. I wasn't sure how to take on such a vast project while still maintaining service as my primary aim.

After years of putting it off due to other priorities in my life and career, everything seemed to fall into place all at once, and I felt it was time to sit down and persevere through it. This book is the product of that effort.

That being said, this project would never have been possible without the help of many individuals:

First, my son Paul, the writer in my family, has offered countless hours listening to my ideas, offering insights and advice, and helping put my thoughts and ideas into words. It has been an incredible experience working with him on this book.

Second, my family, has been invaluable for their encouragement and support—Sherri, Paul, Katie, Ryan, my mom and dad, and my siblings John and Sue (whom, as you'll see, were the basis for our main characters). Especially Sherri and Ryan for their patience and understanding through all the hours I've spent working on this book.

Third, Paul's editor, Lola Dunn, for the hours she spent pouring over this book and the extra insights she has offered along the way.

Lastly, but certainly not least important, I owe a lot of the ideas in this book to my mentors and peers—Matt Zagula, for his strong encouragement and belief in me, Drew Horter for taking the time to read each chapter as I completed it, my invaluable team, Jan and Connie, for all their input, and many others. Without their help, this book would never have happened.

I hope that you will read this book, study it, and take it to heart as you take your own journey into retirement. *The Five Crossroads* can be invaluable to you if you are willing to learn from them. May your journey begin now and always be an enjoyable one.

Chapter I
"The Letter"

It began on a Saturday morning, the sun just peaking over the horizon. John slumped down at his table, exhausted after a long sleepless night. He sipped his orange juice and picked absentmindedly at his toast and jam, speculating about the contents of the mysterious envelope that had arrived in the mail the afternoon before. Try as he might, John couldn't bring himself to open the letter.

The envelope appeared aged and faded, as if mailed many years ago. There was no stamp, no return address, and no mark of an addressee. In fact, the envelope only had five simple yet concerning handwritten words scrawled across the front:

"Is Your Retirement in Danger?"

Truth be told, that same question had been buzzing in John's mind for quite some time. He had worked hard throughout his career, setting aside a savings and investing in the stock market and various retirement accounts. When he retired a few years back, he felt comfortable with the money he'd made from his investments.

John took another sip of orange juice and ran a worried palm through his greying hair above his broad forehead. He nervously fingered the envelope while the question stared up at him, like a warning stop sign that appeared out of nowhere.

John hadn't planned on the market crashing and losing half of his money in the process. Nor had he planned on tax rates increasing while interest rates plummeted. He had poured his heart and soul into the hope that one day the money would come back. But a few years passed and the market never fully recovered.

He had counted on his Social Security, his pension and his retirement accounts to provide enough money for him and his wife, Sue, to live out the remainder of their lives comfortably. He had even dared to hope that perhaps he would be able to leave a little bit behind for his children and a charity or two.

Now it appeared he would have no such luck. He and Sue needed to take a long, hard look at their finances and decide what they could salvage from the wreckage that the economic crash had left in its wake, but they hadn't a clue where to begin.

Sue shuffled into the kitchen in her fuzzy pink bathrobe and comfy slippers. She yawned and smiled at John sympathetically as she crossed the floor and kissed his forehead.

"Couldn't sleep again?" she asked, concerned. John shook his head. He had spent many sleepless nights tossing and turning as he worried about their financial losses.

Sue, who was still a few years away from retirement herself, worried that she wouldn't be able to retire at all in order to keep a steady income. She feared her working years could stretch on much longer than she expected.

She squeezed his hand tightly, sensing the pressure he faced and the stress building. They would be forced to make several sacrifices in the next few years if things didn't turn around.

As Sue returned to her morning routine, shuffling across the kitchen to the fridge, the envelope once again drew John's gaze.

Letting out a deep sigh of resignation, he reluctantly tore the fold of the envelope open and pulled the letter out. They needed help. Similar to the envelope, the paper looked aged and slightly yellow, and the ink seemed to have been penned with a quill. How curious, he thought to himself.

He read:

"Dear John & Sue Smith,

Over half of the retirees in America wish they could have the chance to go back in time and do more planning to be better prepared for retirement.

Today, this makes you very fortunate. Why? Because I am offering you the chance to become better prepared now. No, there is no time machine to take you back before you retired, nor is there any way to undo what has already been done. However, there is a way that you both can reach a better position for the future.

I challenge you to consider what you've just read and to attend an event uniquely catered to your needs at the following address:

123 Retirement Dr.

I have only one thing to ask of you. Please come together. Your financial future concerns both of you. You are a team, and it is always best if you work as such.

There is no cost, but the benefits can be unlimited if you are willing to learn. I promise that if you are open-minded, you can learn things that will change your lives forever."

The letter bore no company insignia and was simply signed *"Your Guide"* at the bottom of the page, adding even more mystery to the letter. John read the letter again, taking in the message, before setting it down on the table.

Was this just another advertising gimmick from a financial advisor, or was it something different altogether? Why hadn't this "Guide" left his name or the name of the company?

Sensing that John was deep in thought, Sue put down her bowl of oatmeal and padded across the room to her husband's side.

"John, dear, what is it?" she asked, placing a hand on his shoulder. "Are you alright?"

"I- I'm fine." He said, unconvincingly. He gnawed thoughtfully on his bottom lip. "Sue, what do you make of this letter?"

Sue lifted her reading glasses from the kitchen table, adjusted them onto the bridge of her nose, and carefully studied the letter.

"My word," she said after reading the letter twice over, "I've never seen anything like this before."

"There's no name, no company and no phone number." John said.

"I suppose it *is* very peculiar." Sue answered as she perused the letter once again.

"I think we should see what it's all about." John said slowly as though thinking aloud. "I mean, what do we have to lose?"

"We have been thinking plenty about what we can do to get out of this financial mess," Sue added. "Maybe this letter is a sign that it's time to take action."

John agreed. This letter seemed to have arrived at the perfect time. He felt a flicker of hope ignite once more. Perhaps this so-called Guide really could help them.

***

Monday Morning...
123 Retirement Drive

As John and Sue pulled into the driveway, he looked down at the address on the letter and then up. Rather than seeing a run-down, one-room office space, he was looking at a quaint, Victorian-style home.

"This can't be it," John said, feeling flabbergasted. "This is someone's home."

"Isn't it peculiar?" Sue asked with girlish excitement in her voice. "I feel as if we've somehow stumbled into the 1800s."

"Well, we've come this far," John said, "let's just go knock on the door and see if this is the right place."

Sue knew her husband was right. They had put off seeking expert advice for far too long. If they went home now, they would most likely forget the whole thing and find themselves right back where they started with their finances: concerned and aimless.

Sensing adventure in the air, John took a moment of mental preparation while helping his wife out of the car. The two walked hand in hand up to the front door. John raised his arm to knock, but the door swung open before he could.

Behind the door, a beautiful young woman greeted them with a warm smile. She ushered them inside and shook their hands invitingly.

"Feel free to take a look around," the young woman said. "We've been expecting you. Your Guide will be right with you."

"He's expecting us?" John asked, incredulous. "You must have us confused with another appointment. This is our first time here and we didn't call ahead."

"It's Mr. and Mrs. Smith, isn't it?" the young woman asked, sitting down at her desk in the corner of the room to confirm her schedule.

John nodded. "John and Sue Smith. Right here."

She turned the computer screen to show them that they were indeed scheduled at the exact moment they stepped in the door.

Sensing their confusion, the young woman tried to put them at ease.

"Your Guide works exclusively with one couple at a time, and only when he is needed," the young woman said with a reassuring smile. "He knows a lot more than just finances. Again, feel free to look around."

Save the young woman's desk, the room was square and empty. Offsetting the sparse appearance, the walls were immaculately decorated. Beautiful velvet-red curtains fringed in gold hung from the windows, and a few Monet paintings graced the walls in glittering, austere frames. On the desk in the corner was a large bouquet of gerbera daisies, Sue's favorite flowers.

"How beautiful." Sue whispered, motioning to the vase. She and John stood speechless for a moment, taking everything in.

After waiting only a few moments, the door in the back opened and a man wearing a suit with a blue tie, John's favorite color, stepped out and smiled at them both.

"Welcome, welcome." The man said, shaking each of their hands warmly. "You must be the Smiths."

"How do you know who we are?" John queried, still curious about the Guide's knowledge of their unscheduled appointment. "We've only just arrived and the secretary didn't even inform you that we were here."

A warm, knowing smile flitted across his face as he turned to the young woman and winked. She returned the smirk without breaking the quick clicks at her keyboard.

"I know who you are because I only send one invitation to my humble establishment at a time. It can only serve

The Five Crossroads

one purpose at a time, after all, and at the present, my services are dedicated only to you."

Recovering from the oddity of the situation, John spoke up. "We were intrigued by your letter and rather curious about what you can do to help us out of our current situation," John said. "I did notice the letter didn't include your name."

"It did, though," the man answered, "I like to refer to myself as your Guide."

John and Sue exchanged questioning looks.

"How mysterious," Sue said.

"Not at all, Mrs. Smith," the man replied. "I am here to guide you and Mr. Smith on a journey that has the potential to change your life. So the title is rather fitting, wouldn't you say?"

"It all sounds intriguing, er..., Mr. Guide." John replied, tentatively.

"Oh, indeed it is, John. Indeed it is," the Guide replied as he strode to a door that seemed to lead further into the house. As he reached the door, his cheery smiled faded into a determined expression.

He took Sue's hand and they watched as the Guide backed up against the door.

"Are you ready to begin your journey, Mr. & Mrs. Smith?" He asked, looking each in the eye as he awaited their answers.

"I suppose we are," John said.

"I want you to be absolutely sure," the Guide replied. "The things you are about to witness will change your life if you let them, forever."

Again, John and Sue looked at one another. This Guide was making quite an impression. They were intrigued.

"Before I open this door," the Guide continued, "I want you to know that many choices lie before you. On this imminent journey, you will come to five crossroads, each representing a critical decision you must make for your retirement plan."

"Crossroads?" Sue asked.

"Yes," the Guide replied. "Each of these crossroads has many paths to follow and no one answer works for everyone. Every individual is different, which means every individual must take a different path in order to arrive at their destination."

"That's why you're here, though, right?" John asked nervously. "You're here to guide us along the right path."

"I am your Guide but I am still limited. You see, I can only tell you where each path will lead you. In order to make the right decision you must know your dreams, your goals, and yourselves."

"I don't understand," Sue said, critically. "You're saying you don't know where to guide us?"

"Imagine you're about to get on to the freeway in Chicago. You can head east toward New York or west toward Los Angeles," the Guide answered. "Imagine, though, that there are no signs and no indication of which way is east or west, north or south."

"How would we know where to go?" Sue asked.

"That is exactly my point," the Guide replied. "That's where I come in. As your Guide, I know the layout of the roads and where each will take you. It's still up to you, however, to tell me where you want to end up."

Sue nodded understandingly.

"Now imagine those highways will take you to your retirement dreams. I do know your names but I still have so much to learn about *you*," the Guide said. "I don't know yet what you want out of your retirement."

John thought for a moment. He hadn't considered his dreams lately because of the ever-present reality of his situ-

The Five Crossroads

ation. It was certainly time to reevaluate what he and Sue wanted out of life.

"For instance, perhaps you want to travel," the Guide said.

"Or golf," John interrupted, excited.

"Or golf, precisely," the Guide replied. "There are so many different ways to live out your retirement, and there is no right or wrong answer. There is only a right or wrong way to get there."

"I see," Sue said, beginning to understand, "so you want us to tell you what we want out of our retirement years, and you'll show us which path will take us there?"

"That's absolutely right, Mrs. Smith," the Guide said. "That's why we developed the five crossroads. We want to determine the best path for you and your specific retirement needs."

The Guide placed his hand on the doorknob and raised his eyebrows mischievously.

"Now, are you absolutely sure that you're ready to take the first step on your journey toward the perfect retirement?"

John offered Sue his arm and they shared a hopeful glance. They were both nervous, but they felt confident that their aimless plans were about to change for the better.

"We're ready," John said firmly.

"Then let us begin." The Guide smiled and swung the door open.

Questions to Consider for Your Retirement

1. How many sleepless nights have you spent worrying about your retirement?
2. How long have you put off planning for your retirement? How much longer can you afford to procrastinate?
3. Are your investments set up properly should the market prove volatile? What if taxes rise? What if interest rates plummet?
4. Have you defined your retirement hopes and dreams? Have you considered that working with a retirement guide can allow you to take the right steps to achieve those dreams?
5. Did you know that every financial situation is unique? Do you have a retirement plan that is specifically tailored to your needs?
6. Are you ready to receive a second opinion that could change your life?
7. Are you ready to start your own retirement journey and change your life?

Notes

Chapter II
"Tea and Taxes"

When the door swung open, the surprised couple stared into an empty room. No furniture decorated the room and the walls were unadorned, save for a single painting centered on the far wall.

The painting was of a very familiar character dressed in a suit of red, white and blue. The man was tipping his blue top hat to commence a bow. He stood in front of a single tree at the center of a crossroad. Both roads seemed to stretch out far away and into the distance. The area was surrounded by fields that were curiously tinged purple. Uncle Sam, in the midst of his bow, seemed to be smiling in gratitude as if receiving a generous gift from each passerby.

"As I'm sure you both already know," the Guide said as he walked up to the painting, "this painting depicts a man named Uncle Sam."

"Oh, we know Uncle Sam," John said, chuckling. Sue laughed as well.

"Of course you do," the Guide replied. "After all, he's an important character in American culture. Are you, however, familiar with the crossroad at which he's standing?" the Guide asked.

"I'm afraid not," John answered as he leaned in to take a closer look.

"That is the **Tax Reduction Crossroad**," the Guide said, pointing to where Uncle Sam stood.

"Tax Reduction?" John asked. "Isn't our CPA in charge of that?"

"Actually, there's a difference between tax preparation and tax planning," the Guide said. "You see, a CPA is in charge of tax preparation. They look backward to see what you've done the year before. Guides like myself look to the future to help you plan the year ahead so you can position yourself for future tax reduction."

"That sounds interesting, but it seems like so much work," John said.

"I can't tell you how many people have told me that exact thing," the Guide said. "You're not the only ones who get a little overwhelmed sometimes. Everyone wants to pay their fair share, but figuring out how to do it can be quite a challenge."

"Well, I see how my taxes are used," John said, with a hint of sarcasm, "and that others aren't paying any taxes at all. It would be nice to know I'm not paying more than necessary."

"Well, I know just the man to help you out," the Guide said.

As John and Sue both inspected the painting more closely, they noticed something very peculiar. It seemed as if a cool summer breeze was blowing gently through the tree and the waving grass within the artwork.

Suddenly, Uncle Sam leaned upright and placed his hat back upon his head.

"Oh my word," Sue exclaimed. "Did that painting just move?"

The Smiths looked back at the Guide to see if their imaginations were running wild or not. The Guide smiled at them both and nodded.

"Look again," he said, pointing at the painting.

The couple turned to scrutinize the painting more closely, but instead they found themselves standing at the crossroad themselves next to Uncle Sam who smiled warm-

The Five Crossroads

ly. Within the painting the summer breeze wafted warmly, rustling the large oak tree in front of them. John and Sue noticed that the tall grass was indeed a deep lavender color.

"Well, I guess it's safe to say we're not in Kansas anymore," John said, amazed.

"Good day to the both of you," Uncle Sam boomed pleasantly, shaking their hands, giving them a firm grip on the reality of the place.

"How is this possible?" John asked, looking around at the scenery which, only moments ago, had been just a lovely painting. "I must be dreaming."

"We get that a lot in these parts," Uncle Sam said. "And what a pleasant dream it is, if I may say so myself. The sun is shining and the tree just looks beautiful this time of year, doesn't it?"

John nodded slowly, still bewildered by what had just happened. Sue, also overwhelmed, held his arm listlessly as she gazed at her surroundings.

"Well, folks, I didn't mean to eavesdrop on your conversation with the Guide out there but, well, I am in a painting, and it can get awfully lonely," Uncle Sam said with a joking smile. "I believe you were mentioning your fear of paying too much in taxes."

"That's right," John replied. "I'm proud to be an American, and I'm more than happy to pay my fair share. I just feel like I may be paying too much."

"It's funny you should use those words," Uncle Sam said, "'fair share.' I've heard those words before."

John looked puzzled.

"Well, I could explain the importance of paying your fair share, but I'd rather have someone more familiar discuss it," Uncle Sam replied vaguely. "Follow me."

He led the Smiths along one of the roads that forked away from them. As they followed, John and Sue noticed the atmosphere and setting changing and shifting with every passing step. It was if the world wound back through time. Night suddenly descended and a cold winter chill crept in with the wind.

They came to a crowded harbor where the people, dressed in traditional colonial garb and also Indian disguises, rushed about with a tempo of purpose and excitement.

"Why are they hurrying?" John asked, trying to warm his nearly frozen hands. Just at that moment, one of the men stopped in his tracks when he spotted them.

Atop his head was a white wig with a short ponytail trailing from the back, decorated with Indian feathers. He walked over to them and studied John for a moment before smiling vibrantly and throwing his arms around him.

"Oh John, I thought it was you! Boy, you've grown up to be quite a good looking man," the stranger exclaimed over the commotion, hugging John as if they were old friends. "I guess it must be those Smith genes."

"I'm sorry, have we met?" John queried uncertainly.

"Dear me, no," the man answered, chuckling, "but I check in on you every once in a while. I'm your great-great-great...ah, well, you get the idea."

"You're..." John started.

"That's right, John," the man replied, saluting, "Linus T. Smith at your service."

"This is incredible," John said. "I've read the accounts in your journals about the amazing things you did during history."

Suddenly, a loud cheer rose up from a concentrated crowd near the docks.

"Well, you're about to witness history in the making," Linus said. "Welcome to the Boston Tea Party."

John and Sue surveyed the milling crowd as best they could in the moonlight until they spotted several groups of

The Five Crossroads

men dressed as Native Americans standing on the decks of three ships, heaving crates into the sea below.

"Wow!" John breathed, squeezing his wife's hand excitedly. "Can you believe it? We've heard this story so many times, but to actually see it happen."

They watched for a moment, their breath puffing in the air, as the men whooped and hollered like bandits as they destroyed the taxed tea in the murky ocean below.

"Look there," Linus said, pointing at one of the ships. "That man is Paul Revere. He's a gentleman I'm sure you'll recognize. Oh, isn't this exciting?"

"It is," John exclaimed. "So, that's Paul Revere? This is incredible."

John glanced over to see several men in British uniforms tossing the tea overboard. "Who are those men over there in uniform?"

"Those men?" Linus asked. "That's the captain and the British sailors. After we explained that we didn't want to hurt anyone, the captain and his men were happy to help."

"That's a lot of tea," Sue said, looking into the ocean.

"You're right," Linus said. "Were you aware that the tea on these three vessels costs around *one million dollars*? That's over twelve million dollars in your time."

"Wow," John said through chattering teeth. "I can't believe we're actually here."

"Where are my manners? Quick, let's get you two inside before you catch your death of cold." Linus ushered the chilled couple into a nearby cabin warmed by a glowing fire. "There, that's better. Well, I hear you're in the middle of your own tax debate. Anything I can do to help?"

"Well," John said, rubbing his hands together, "we're meeting with a man who calls himself the Guide and he briefly mentioned tax reduction. We'd like to reduce our taxes if we could."

"Sounds like a good idea to me," Linus said.

"It is. I just don't know where to start," John said, thinking of the tea crates floating in the water. "It's not that I want to be unpatriotic. I'm happy to lend my support to this great country. I just want to pay my fair share."

"John, these men didn't know where to start either," Linus stated. "That's why they stood up and fought for the right to pay only their fair share. Reducing your taxes isn't taking advantage of the government; it's just making sure that you're not paying more than you should."

"Really?" John asked, intrigued.

"That's right," Linus said. "We threw the tea over the sides of the ships because we didn't want to pay taxes to someone overseas who never bothered to listen to our opinions."

"I suppose that makes sense," John said. "I don't want to pay less than I ought to either, though."

"Absolutely not," Linus answered. "You live in a country built by stalwart founding fathers dedicated to sustaining freedoms. Freedoms such as these are not only worth fighting for, but paying for too."

John nodded in agreement.

"That's why Uncle Sam here and the rest of the United States government have given you the freedom to make use of certain tax laws that can save you money. They're allowing you to keep what's rightfully yours," Linus said. "But they're not going to go through every American's personal finances and find these savings for them. You have to stand up for what's yours. That's what a true patriot does. Tell him Sam."

Uncle Sam nodded and held up two very large books that seemed to have appeared from thin air and thumped them down on a nearby table.

The Five Crossroads

"These books are today's United States tax code. These books contain 1,000 pages and nearly half a million words each."

John and Sue's eyes grew wide in amazement at the size of the books.

"These pages contain laws that can show you several credits, deductions and exemptions that you may not even know apply to you."

"That's so much to read to save just a little bit each year," John said, shocked.

"First, that little bit adds up over time," Uncle Sam replied. "If you were able to save $2,500 a year, for example, it wouldn't just apply to that year. Every year after, you would save that same $2,500. Over ten years, you could have an extra $25,000, and so on. An extra $2,500 dollars a year can change your whole retirement lifestyle."

"I guess I didn't see it that way before," John said. "That'd be an extra vacation every year."

"That's right," Uncle Sam continued. "Secondly, when it comes to reading, I couldn't agree with you more. It's time-intensive work to read these books. That's why people like your Guide exist."

"What do you mean?" John asked.

"Well, as you said, it's an extensive amount of reading," Uncle Sam said, "and the technicalities are difficult to understand. That's why retirement guides exist: to constantly study and learn not only what these laws *are*, but also what they *mean*."

John and Sue still felt perplexed.

"You wouldn't expect to read a couple of books on architecture and then feel prepared to build your own skyscraper, would you? Retirement guidance is the same way. Reading one or two books doesn't make you an expert. A lifetime of study and time spent in the industry teaches you how to stay on top of these laws," Uncle Sam said.

Sue nodded thoughtfully, as the fire crackled away in the hearth. They were feeling warmer by the minute.

"These books are here for your advantage," Uncle Sam said. "They were written in order to help you take more control of the taxes you pay."

"That's good," Sue said.

"There's a lot of new information to keep up with, however," Uncle Sam continued. "It's not impossible to see several new tax law changes. It's been done before and it could easily be done again. How many more pages would that be for you to have to read?"

"Quite a few," John replied, chuckling.

"It sounds like a full-time job," Sue added.

"It is," Uncle Sam replied. "That's the career that retirement guides chose. They wanted to help good, honest, hard-working Americans like yourself by keeping up with these laws to save you the time and hassle."

"I guess it's best to rely on someone who has dedicated the time it takes to stay up-to-date on these things," John said.

"That's right," Linus said, cutting in. "Listen, John, you're a good man. I can see that you're proud of being an American, and you carry a bit of the Boston Tea Party fire with you.

You take care of yourself and protect what's rightfully yours. The IRS will always get their fair share."

Linus hugged them both and smiled.

"It was an honor to meet you," he said.

"Are you leaving?" John asked.

"No, I have a tea party to attend," Linus replied, "but you two must be on your way. Uncle Sam has a lot more to

The Five Crossroads

share with you. I know you're going to enjoy the rest of your journey. Good luck and farewell."

When Linus had left the cabin, a thick fog enveloped the little house in what seemed like only a few moments. When it lifted, John's ancestor, the room, the frosty night, and the entire harbor had disappeared with it, leaving only another path.

Uncle Sam looked at them both, reading the surprise on their faces.

"Shall we continue?" he asked.

John and Sue nodded excitedly.

"Lead on," John said, taking his wife's hand in his.

Questions to Consider for Your Retirement

1. Are you paying more than your fair share in taxes?
2. How much money could you save this year by reducing your taxes? How much money would you save over 10 years or 20 years? What options would become possible with that extra money?
3. Do you understand the difference between tax planning and tax preparation?
4. Do you understand the intricacies of the U.S. Tax Code? Are you taking advantage of all the credits, deductions and exemptions available to you?

Notes

Chapter III
"The Four Pails"

Uncle Sam led the Smiths down the new path. As they walked, the empty country surrounding them transformed into fields and crops with livestock grazing here and there.

"I trust your journey has been interesting so far?" Uncle Sam asked archly.

"Interesting?" Sue exclaimed. "It's been amazing! There's a surprise around every turn."

"Well, I'm glad you don't mind the surprises!" Uncle Sam exclaimed with an air of mystery.

They continued on until they came to another crossroad. Two paths stretched out before them, one leading to the left and the other leading right.

A fenced field stood ahead of them with a few cows resting in the sun. A large old-fashioned barn stood near the fence with the door ajar. Occasional moos came in a stream from the open door. Uncle Sam nodded at them and casually climbed over the fence into the field.

"This is the place," he said, helping Sue clamber over and then turning back to help John. "I have something very important to share with you. You know why reducing taxes is important, but now you need to learn how it can be done."

Uncle Sam led them to the barn and ushered them in. A warm, distinct animal smell rose up to meet them at the doorway. A few rows of stalls stood along each side of the barn with a cow standing in each one. Amidst the stomps and lowing, a man's voice rang out.

"Well, howdy folks!" said a voice coming from beneath the closest cow. "I'll be done here in just a minute. I was just finishing the mornin' milkin'." After a moment, a farmer in faded blue overalls stood up to shake their hands. "Using my barn for another presentation, eh Uncle Sam?" he asked archly.

"Aw Melvin, you know the routine," Uncle Sam said with a laugh in his voice. "John and Sue here are ready to learn, but we simply can't go on without those milk pails."

"Milk pails?" John and Sue shared a questioning glance.

"Shucks, I'm just happy to oblige," Melvin replied. "Y'all have fun and don't mind the cows; they always appreciate the guests." With that, he strode out the barn door.

"Well folks, it may not be much, but it's at least a way to rest your feet." Uncle Sam gestured to a few squat three-legged stools on the floor as seats.

Sue thanked him and sat down as delicately as possible while Uncle Sam went to a series of nails on the walls and took down four milk pails. Sam crouched down and began to organize the milk pails upright in a row.

"Melvin just offered us a great example. Imagine milking cows represents your career," Uncle Sam said. "That means that the milk is the money you make. Each of these pails represents a type of account in which you can invest your money."

Examining the pails more closely, they could see that three of them were dotted with various holes.

The first pail looked as if it had been destroyed by a shotgun. There were holes scattered everywhere from top to bottom.

"This pail," Uncle Sam said, "represents a taxable account. It could be a savings account, a CD, money markets, and other types of investments."

The Five Crossroads

"We have some of those," Sue admitted, pointing at the pail.

"Of course you do," Uncle Sam said. "It's important that you store a little bit of your money in accounts like these. That way, you have access to your money whenever you need it. Personally, I recommend having a minimum of three to twelve months of income put into an account like this to which you always have immediate access."

"Why is it filled with holes?"

"It goes back to the tax code," Uncle Sam said. "With these accounts, your money can leak out. You're giving away more than your fair share as you said earlier, John."

"I don't get taxed a lot on these accounts. Why is that considered too much?" John asked.

"Well, you've already paid taxes on the money in these accounts," Uncle Sam replied. "Now you're going to be taxed on the interest and dividends. That means less money in your pockets and more in the pockets of the IRS."

Uncle Sam slowly began filling the pail with some fresh milk. The milk instantly poured through the holes. "See, at this rate, a portion of your money pours out as you accumulate it."

"I guess we have a bit more in those types of pails than we probably should," John conceded, looking at the mess on the floor.

"Again, there's nothing wrong with having a little money in taxable accounts," Uncle Sam said. "You just want to make sure you take control of your money, and your retirement guide is there to help. He wants to help you pay fewer taxes so you can spend your money on the person who deserves it most: you."

"What's the second pail?" Sue asked, glancing down the line. Just like the first, it had holes; however, there weren't as many, and the holes only covered the bottom half of the pail.

"This pail represents your tax-deferred accounts. This can be your IRA, your 401(k), select bonds, annuities and some other types of investments."

"We have some money in those, too," John mentioned.

"Good," Uncle Sam said, "because there are several benefits to these types of accounts."

"What kinds of benefits?"

"When you contribute money into many of these accounts, you are allowed to deduct your contributions from your taxable income."

"That's true."

"And, of course, all your gains are tax-deferred until you make a withdrawal."

"That's right," John said brightly, thinking back to when he set up his IRA. "I don't have to pay taxes on those until I take the money out myself. They'll force me to do it anyway, though, at 70½, right?"

"Therein lies the catch," Uncle Sam answered. He strode over to the barn door and gestured widely to the fields outside.

In the distance, John and Sue could see Melvin in the next field planting seeds.

"Unfortunately, these types of accounts become a tax time bomb. Because you were willing to defer the tax on your seeds you are accountable to pay the tax on the crops that grow from them."

"I don't understand," John said.

As an example Uncle Sam moved back to the pail to fill it with milk. Initially the drain was slow, but as the pail filled, the milk poured even faster. "It's not uncommon for an account like this to double or even triple in size. Sometimes it can grow even larger than that," Uncle Sam said.

The Five Crossroads

"The larger your account gets, the larger the tax drain is. Also, guess what bigger accounts mean for our unsuspecting taxpayer?"

"Higher tax brackets."

"Exactly," Uncle Sam exclaimed. "It's not always the case but it's more common than you'd think."

"Then I'm guessing we want the majority of our money in another pail," John mused.

"Now wait a second," Uncle Sam said. "These accounts are much better than the accounts in the first pail, or the taxable accounts. Even after paying the tax, you'll wind up with more than you would with the same investment built up in a regular taxable account."

"Alright," John said.

"That's why you can work closely with a guide who can review your options," Uncle Sam explained. "He can show you how to start moving your money from the taxable pail to the other pails."

"To improve our situation?" John asked.

"That's right," Uncle Sam replied.

"Okay, I get it now," John said, nodding. One of the cows added a loud moo in agreement. John and Sue chuckled.

"The third pail, as you can see, is in even better shape than the second pail," Uncle Sam said, holding it up for the Smiths to see.

This pail had a few holes near the top instead of the bottom like the second pail had.

"This third pail represents tax-free accounts."

"Like a Roth IRA?" Sue asked.

"That's right," Uncle Sam replied, "but Roth IRAs are only one of many types. Tax-free accounts are any type of account where you pay taxes on the money going in but not at any future time. The growth and income aren't taxed."

Sue interjected cautiously, "I'm sure I'm going to feel foolish for asking but if this pail is tax-free, why are there still holes in it, and why doesn't the fourth pail have any holes? What could be better than tax-free?"

"There is no such thing as a foolish question. Asking questions means you're willing to learn. You'll always have plenty of questions for your guide, after all."

Sue smiled appreciatively.

"To answer your question," Uncle Sam continued, "many people believe that because their money is in tax-free accounts they will never have to worry about taxes again."

"And that's not true?" John asked.

"Well, yes and no," Uncle Sam replied. "When you pass away, the estate tax takes over. You won't have to worry about taxes again but your children might."

"What's the estate tax?" Sue asked.

"Retirement guides call it the 'death' tax," Uncle Sam said. "When you pass away, the government may or may not tax your estate based on its size."

John's eyes lit up. "So the fourth pail must be-"

"That's right John," Uncle Sam said. "The fourth pail represents accounts that are set up properly so as to protect your money from the estate tax."

"So that's where we want our money to be?" John asked.

"As much as possible, yes," Uncle Sam replied, "but don't completely discount the others. Each pail plays an important part in your complete financial portfolio, and that's why it's important to have the right guide."

John looked at his wife and smiled thoughtfully. They'd learned a lot so far, just at this first crossroad.

"I can see that the two of you have a lot to discuss," Uncle Sam surmised, "but that's why working with a guide that you trust is so important. Your guide can help you maximize the potential of your portfolio by showing you the

The Five Crossroads

right amount to put in each pail. The right guide can do so much more for you as well. Remember, the Tax Reduction crossroad is only the first of the five crossroads."

"You mean there's more?" Sue asked.

"Well, of course there's more," Uncle Sam said. "There's so much more."

Questions to Consider for Your Retirement

1. Do you understand the four pails of monetary storage and the difference between each (Taxable, Tax-Deferred, Tax-Free, Tax-Free/Estate Tax-Free)?
2. Do you have a minimum of three to twelve months of income set aside for emergencies or immediate needs?
3. Are your estate and investments set up to avoid the estate tax?
4. Are your current retirement investments a ticking tax bomb? What are you doing to avoid paying too much in taxes?
5. Are you putting off paying tax on the seeds and are you aware that by doing so you will have to pay more on the crop?
6. Are you maximizing the potential of your retirement portfolio by placing the right amount of your assets into each of the four pails?

Notes

Chapter IV
"The Three-Legged Stool"

The three of them stood close in the barn while John and Sue waited for something magical to happen. They were met only by the soft lowing of the cows in the pasture.

"Where do we go from here?" John asked.

"Well," Uncle Sam said, "We're off to meet an old friend of mine to help us continue the journey."

"Really, who is it?" Sue asked, excitedly hoping the next visitor would prove to be just as extraordinary as the others.

"You'll just have to wait and see," Uncle Sam said. "Come on, we've got quite a walk ahead of us."

The three of them strode out of the barn and out to the path leading left of the crossroad.

"While we walk, I'd like to share a few things with you," Uncle Sam said.

"Okay," John replied.

"Let me ask you something," Uncle Sam began, setting a brisk pace. "What are your concerns when it comes to retirement?"

John and Sue both thought for a moment.

"I guess one main concern is whether or not we will have enough money in retirement to last us the rest of our lives," John said, tripping a bit to catch up.

"That's a big one," Uncle Sam said. "It's hard to imagine what life would be like if the money runs out."

"Life would be a lot harder," Sue said.

"It would, wouldn't it?" Uncle Sam considered. "You don't want to outlive your money. In a perfect world, we'd spend the last of our money on our way out the door, but we can't predict that final day."

"I guess not," John chuckled. "That's true, though. It would be nice to spend your last penny on your last meal."

They laughed at the thought as the scenery again began to change. The grass shortened along the path, and more dry dirt appeared. The sun beat down a bit more fiercely. John wiped his forehead, and Sue began fanning her face.

"There's something else to take into account too. People are living longer than they ever have in the past," Uncle Sam said. "In fact, according to studies, one out of two people live to age 90. Well, we're just about here!"

John and Sue stopped abruptly to see where they were. They found themselves on a dusty street winding down the center of a row of little shacks. The shacks looked homemade, fashioned out of wooden planks, aluminum boards, and other scraps. Several men slept casually against buildings, a few children scampered and laughed through the houses, and the clink of pots and pans chimed out from within the shacks. A man in a dusty wheelchair rolled down the road and gave Uncle Sam a friendly wave as they approached. He maneuvered into a nearby shack for a moment.

Sue's eyes widened in sudden clarity. "Oh, Sam. Are we where I think we are?" she asked tentatively, hugging John's arm.

"Yes, Sue. I believe you know just where we are, Uncle Sam said with gravity in his voice. "This is the Great Depression, 1935. These were certainly some dark years for America indeed. But don't fret too much. These communi-

The Five Crossroads

ties manage to scrape by with a lot of heart and even more hope that things will get better."

"Ha! Mainly because they can't get any worse," a bright voice shouted from the shack. The man in the wheelchair emerged from the shack with a grin, carrying a three-legged stool, similar to the ones they had seen in the barn.

"Sam, I thought we talked about this," the man laughed as he wheeled himself down the lane. "We can't keep holding these meetings in this dusty town. My wheelchair can't take it much longer."

"I'm sorry sir," Uncle Sam said, walking over to maneuver him close to John and Sue. "It just works so well for what you want to teach our friends."

"I know, I know," the man said, brushing off his worn, black suit. "By the way, John, Sue, welcome to the **Retirement Income Crossroad**. My name is-"

"President Roosevelt," John said, recognizing the man right away, "it is an honor to meet you."

"You see that, Sam," the man said, turning to Uncle Sam and giving his arm a playful shake, "my reputation precedes me."

"Indeed," Uncle Sam laughed as the man in the wheelchair turned his attention back to the Smiths.

"It's a pleasure to meet you both," the man said, wheeling over and shaking John's hand, then Sue's. "President Franklin Delano Roosevelt, at your service."

"What are you doing here, Mr. President?" John asked, as a group of men in tattered jeans walked by and waved. "This isn't exactly the place I would expect you to be."

"I often stop by to see how my country is really fairing. I've worked long and hard to create new work programs to get good men out of places like this and into gainful employment again," Roosevelt said with emotion in his voice.

After a moment's pause, he continued, "As a bonus, I'm here to talk to you about Retirement Income."

"Sir," Uncle Sam said, "we've just been discussing one of their biggest retirement concerns."

"Yes, yes, having enough money to last," President Roosevelt said knowingly.

"How did you know?" Sue asked.

"It was the same concern the retirees and those about to retire had in my time," he replied with a sign, "besides being worried about having enough money at all."

"What did you do?" Sue asked.

"Glad you asked," the President said. "It was 1935, just this time of year, in fact. We were nearing the end of the Great Depression, and people were in bad financial shape. I felt they needed a reason to start saving again. I wanted to help them.

"I signed the Social Security Act, and it helped that generation save something for retirement." Another group walked past with smiles of appreciation on their faces. "These good people needed it, and the bill helped them out quite a lot. The plan backfired later, though. Instead of offering an opportunity to save for retirement, the hardworking Americans of later generations began to depend on Social Security as their entire income during their retirement years.

"That's why it's not doing so well in your current economy. Almost anyone, under the right circumstances, can qualify for Social Security benefits." President Roosevelt paused to let that fact sink in.

"Social Security was originally meant to give people an opportunity by offering them a supplemental income for retirement," he continued. "It was never intended to replace their income altogether or offer a cushion for disabilities." He shook his head sadly.

The Five Crossroads

"Well, the government has misused the program as well," John said, cutting in.

"You're absolutely right," President Roosevelt replied. "The U.S. government is not free of blame either. I promised that as long as I lived, the people would never pay income tax on their Social Security benefits. It was 1983, several years after I passed away mind you, that Congress changed my program and started taxing Social Security after all. Ten years later, they raised the tax rate. Did you know that currently the government taxes up to 85% of your Social Security check?"

"Wow, really?" John asked. "Even though income is always taxed, that percentage seems too high."

"I certainly agree with you. Especially since you have already had your Social Security taxed when that check arrives," President Roosevelt said. "Let's return to the milk pail analogy Uncle Sam explained. The government is adding more holes to your pails with the current Social Security program."

"That's true," John said. "I hadn't connected those two."

"The real problem is, no matter where the finger of blame is pointing, it doesn't make a difference," the President said. "Either way the Social Security program is in trouble right now. I don't think it will ever disappear, but there's a chance that, in the near future, people may receive fewer benefits, retire later, or the government will tax up to 100% of the Social Security check."

The President rolled his wheelchair over to the stool, picked it up, and set it down in front of the Smiths. As he did so, Uncle Sam offered other stools for the Smiths to sit on. President Roosevelt reached over the small wooden stool and twisted one of the legs loose. He pulled it free and the stool tipped a bit, falling on its side.

"This stool represents the three types of income you'll rely on in your retirement years. The leg I've removed is Social Security because, as I mentioned before, you can't rely upon this program as your sole source of income. It functions as a supplement."

"This one represents your pension," he stated, motioning to another of the wooden legs. "Let me ask, do either of you have a pension?"

"We do," Sue answered, "but it's a small one."

"You're lucky to have one at all," President Roosevelt said, "pensions are slowly disappearing from the workplace in America."

They nodded thoughtfully.

"By the way, I noticed neither of you mentioned a concern about the income available for your spouse if you should pass away. It's something not many people consider, but it's a very important step in putting together a retirement plan."

"What do you mean?" John asked, perplexed. "When I pass away, Sue will have everything that's mine."

"Not everything," the President replied. "You see, when one of you passes away, the other is left with something a bit more complicated. First, whoever survives the other will only get the highest paying Social Security check. The income from the other will be lost. As far as pensions, depending on how you've set them up, either of you could be left with just a portion or nothing at all after your spouse is gone."

"Wow," John said, "I guess we never thought that deeply about it."

"Not many people do I'm afraid," President Roosevelt responded. "It's hard to think about the technicalities surrounding a spouse passing away."

The Five Crossroads

Sue reached over and squeezed John's hand tightly. He looked at her and smiled reassuringly.

"But it's also something important to consider. After all, either one of you could lose a lot of the income you were counting on for the future. On top of that, you could leave your spouse in a higher tax bracket since one of you will be filing as a single person again. Depending on your income, your taxes could go up."

"Oh my," Sue said, looking at her husband. "It seems like we have a lot more planning to do."

As her husband nodded his agreement, President Roosevelt reached over to the stool and loosened another leg, pulling it free. The stool rolled a bit to the side before settling in front of the Smiths.

"Take it from me and from the time I lived in; planning ahead is the most important step now so you can handle those unexpected crises, such as market crashes, that suddenly occur," the President said, gesturing to the shacks around him. "Don't get me wrong; I don't want you to lose faith in Social Security or your pension. I simply want you to put more faith, time and effort into the only leg that gives you complete control."

"The third leg?" John asked.

"That's right," President Roosevelt said, "the third leg is your own savings and investments. The most important thing you need to know about the savings and investments leg is that you can't afford to go backwards."

"Go backwards?" John asked.

"I mean that you want to protect the money you already have before you worry about making more. Losing the money you've worked your entire life to save would be devastating. Even if you never make another dime, you want to make sure that the money you already have is safe and secure."

"That's true," Sue said, "John has been losing a lot of sleep these past few months, worried about the investments we've lost."

"It's extremely difficult to lose money you've already earned," the President reached for the stool once more and unscrewed the third leg. "Without your personal savings and investments, you would lose the last of your support in your retirement years."

He dropped the wooden disk to the ground where it rolled and wobbled to a stop, lying still on the dusty road.

"As long as the savings leg is secure," President Roosevelt said as he reassembled the stool, "you can count on the other two to help support the weight of your lifestyle, but this third leg is critical."

"So it's best to focus on our own retirement accounts?" Sue asked.

"Of course," the President said, "you have no control over your pension or Social Security so your focus should be on taking care of your own accounts."

Sue nodded thoughtfully.

"More importantly, it's critical that you work closely with the right guide to position those retirement accounts exactly where they need to be in order for you to live your retirement years to the fullest." The President took a look around and began his good-byes. "Well, my new friends, it's been a pleasure. I have some visits to make, so I'll wish you luck on your continuing journey."

"Thank you so much Mr. Roosevelt. This has been quite a wake-up call." John and Sue smiled at one another. They had learned so much today, but little could they imagine that so much more still lay ahead.

Questions to Consider for Your Retirement

1. Did you know that half of all Americans will live into their 90s? Do you have enough income to last the rest of your life if you live to be 100?
2. If Social Security benefits are reduced, will you still be able to maintain your current lifestyle? What if the IRS begins taxing up to 100% of your Social Security check? What would you do then?
3. At what rate is your Social Security taxed? What have you done to decrease that tax?
4. Is your three-legged stool stable? Are you working closely with a guide that can help you position your investments so that you can live out your dreams in retirement?
5. How much income will your spouse lose when you pass away? How will it affect his or her tax bracket? Would your spouse still be taken care of?

Notes

Chapter V
"Cornerstone Construction"

After saying farewell to President Roosevelt, Uncle Sam and the Smiths continued on their journey.

As they left the dusty heat behind, John and Sue felt more confident with every passing step. They were excited to learn more so they could live the retirement they'd always imagined.

It wasn't long before the dirt path was obscured by a thick blanket of fog so thick they couldn't see what lay ahead. As quickly as the fog came, it disappeared again and they found themselves in the center of a quiet suburban street.

Many houses lined each side of the street, but they weren't just ordinary houses. John and Sue felt that they had wandered down the white rabbit's hole into Wonderland. Some of the houses were stout and wide with flat, long roofs and exaggerated doorways with wide knobs. Others seemed to be stories and stories tall with steep, sloping roofs and giant sized windows. The mansions on the street were as ornate as palaces, complete with gargoyle statues and marble pillars. Still more seemed just big and wide enough for a single person to fit through. Though they all sat side by side, each one differed from the next.

"I've never seen anything like it," Sue said. "Every single one is different."

"Oh, and you won't find anything quite like this neighborhood either. It's located at the corner of our next crossroad, the **Risk Management Crossroad**," Uncle Sam said. "This is the retirement world, and no one's financial house will look anything like another. Everyone's situation and needs are different. That's why I've brought you here."

"To show us our financial house?" John asked.

"No," Uncle Sam replied, "you're not here to see your financial house; you're here because you're going to build it."

"Build it?" Sue asked.

"Yes," Uncle Sam said, "and I've asked someone you already know to help."

As he said this, he stopped on the road and motioned toward an empty house lot, ready for construction. On the lot, a man in a suit, a lively blue tie and a construction hat leaned over some blueprints, studying them intently at a small workbench. He looked up as if startled as they approached.

"Oh, John and Sue," the man said, smiling. "It's wonderful to see you again. I trust the journey has been ideal thus far?" It was the Guide.

"More than ideal," John answered, "this journey has taught us so much about our retirement that we never could have figured out on our own."

"Excellent!" the Guide said, looking at Uncle Sam and winking.

Uncle Sam laughed.

"I'll leave you to it then," he said as he patted John's back softly. "I have other matters to attend to, but I hope to see you again before your journey's end."

"You're leaving?" Sue asked, disappointed.

The Five Crossroads

"I'm afraid I must. You two aren't the only ones who don't understand the tax laws," Uncle Sam replied with a chuckle.

"We know a little more now, thanks to you," John said.

John and Sue shook Uncle Sam's hand, and he disappeared down the street from which they'd come.

"Well then, are you ready to build your financial house?" the Guide asked, holding out a hard hat for each of them.

"We are," John said with a resolute nod, placing his firmly on his head. Sue gingerly placed hers on as well after smoothing out her hair.

"Alright, before we even begin digging, I'd like to ask you a question about risk."

"Okay," John said hesitantly.

"In your opinion, what is risk?" the Guide asked.

"I suppose it's the danger of losing money in the market," John replied. Sue nodded in agreement.

"That's almost right," the Guide said. "Instead, it's any exposure to the chance of loss. You see, risk isn't only about the market. There's much more to it."

"I guess I never thought about it that way. I always related risk only to my investments."

"Oh yes. It's related to your investments as well," the Guide said. "When it deals with your financial house, though, risk is being exposed to the chance of any loss."

John nodded thoughtfully.

"There are two ways that you can look at risk as it relates to your retirement. One is exposing yourselves to the loss of your money. Another is exposing yourselves to the loss of your assets."

"I'm not sure I understand," John said.

"That's why I'm here to lend a hand as you build your house," the Guide said, motioning to a shovel leaning against the side of the workbench.

"You really want us to build a house?" Sue asked. "We don't have time for that!"

"Oh, it will be quicker than you think," the Guide said. "After all, hasn't today been full of surprises?"

"Okay," John said, "we've come this far. Let's give it a try." He rolled up his sleeves.

"That won't be necessary," the Guide said, "you see, this is a financial house and construction works a little differently."

"What do you mean?" John asked, confused.

"When it comes to your retirement," the Guide answered, "you are always taking a risk. You take risks every day of your life with or without the market, whether you want to or not."

"What kinds of risks?" Sue asked.

"That's a great question." The Guide smiled at her and turned his attention to the empty plot of land behind him.

"First," he said, motioning to the site, "just like literal house construction, your financial house must be built upon a foundation. At each corner of the foundation are cornerstones. These four cornerstones are what hold the foundation in place."

John nodded approvingly.

"Let's start with the first cornerstone: savings," the Guide said. "It's recommended that you have a minimum of three to twelve months of income set aside for immediate or emergency use. This is critical to holding your foundation in place."

As he spoke, John and Sue watched as a cornerstone materialized on the plot of land, solidifying instantly before their eyes.

The Five Crossroads

"Each cornerstone protects you from a different type of risk. This particular cornerstone protects you from many risks that might affect your money. If for any reason you need money quickly, you can depend on this cornerstone to provide that support.

"It is especially useful in an emergency since you have access to those funds immediately, instead of pulling funds from your retirement account, which can take a little extra time."

"I see," John said. "I guess I never considered emergencies as risks."

"So, this 'cornerstone' protects us from unexpected expenses or emergencies that come up?" Sue asked.

"That's absolutely right, Mrs. Smith," the Guide said. "This cornerstone serves as foundational protection against emergencies."

John quickly took a mental inventory of their savings accounts.

"The second cornerstone," the Guide continued, "is equally important."

"What is it?" John asked.

"If it's alright by you, I'd like to introduce you to another one of my friends," the Guide said. "Perhaps if he shares his story with you, he'll help you understand the second cornerstone."

The Guide turned and pointed down the street where they could see a strange vehicle approaching. The contraption was a mix between a very new carriage and a very old car. It had carriage-style large wheels and an open top, but it was not drawn forward by any horses, but rather putted along down the street emitting a good deal of coal smoke. A brass steering wheel jutted out in front of a driver in a suit, whose long legs appeared scrunched up against his body like a frog. He wore a stovepipe hat atop his head and a brilliant black suit to match. A scruffy black beard covered his chin and trailed below his prominent cheek bones.

As the buggy sputtered closer, both John and Sue gasped as soon as they recognized the man. Like many other characters the Smiths had seen today, this man needed no introduction.

"How do you do?" the man asked as the buggy eased to a stop and he clambered down from the seat. He removed his hat and held it to his side respectfully as he shook their hands. "My name is Abraham Lincoln."

"Oh, we know who you are, Mr. President," John said, excitedly, "It's an honor to meet you. My name is John Smith and this is my wife, Sue."

"Why thank you. It's a pleasure to be here to help," President Lincoln replied.

After exchanging pleasantries, he turned and looked at the Smiths' traveling companion for a moment before placing his hat back on his head.

"Hello, my old friend," the President said.

The Guide greeted him warmly.

"John, Sue, I'm here to talk to you about the second cornerstone," the President said, turning his attention back to the Smiths. "This cornerstone is important when it comes to protecting yourself from property risks. You see, this cornerstone represents home and auto insurance."

John and Sue looked thoughtful.

"You have these modern horseless carriages," President Lincoln said. "When I was alive, this model was about to become the newest automobile on the market," he said as he proudly tapped the driver's seat. "All we had were steam powered automobiles and horse-drawn carriages—nothing as spectacular or efficient as your modern-day car.

"However, that same efficiency has also made traveling a dangerous feat. It's important that you protect yourself

The Five Crossroads

from damages—either damage you inflict upon another car or the damage another car inflicts upon yours."

"Especially with some of those teenagers on the road," John said, chuckling.

"Ah, young people," President Lincoln said, sharing in John's laughter. "I had hoped they would be better behaved in your generation."

"Not at all," the Guide said, chiming in.

"That's all the more reason to protect yourselves from those potential losses," President Lincoln said. "Relying upon your own finances to repair or buy a new automobile could take its toll. Accidents are bound to happen, though. They can happen to any of us, so it's best to be prepared."

"You're right," John said.

"Home insurance is equally important," the President added. "After all, your home is either the most or second most valuable asset you will ever own. I purchased an insurance policy on my home in Springfield, Illinois, in 1861 from The Hartford.

"You see, 1861 was a big year for me. It was the year that I became President, and it was the year the Civil War began. I faced a lot of exposure to risk in those days. I had a lot to lose and I felt the insurance policy was an important step in protecting my family from the financial ruin that could have been caused by those losses."

"I suppose you're right," John said.

"It's just as critical for you and Sue to protect your home with proper coverage as well," President Lincoln added. "There are so many natural disasters that can cause irreparable damage to homes. In fact, that's why your foundation is so important."

"That makes sense," John said. "If we have enough money in savings, and we insure our home and car properly against risk, we'll have a solid foundation."

The second cornerstone materialized adjacent to the other and strengthened the foundation. John and Sue smiled at the progress they'd made.

"Not so fast, you two," the Guide said, "we're only halfway there. Remember, these are only two of the cornerstones. There are four cornerstones in a financial house's foundation."

"What are the last two?" Sue asked.

"I'm glad you asked," the Guide replied. "The third cornerstone represents life insurance.

"Life insurance is important to have when you're young because, should something happen early, you want to be able to cover the payments on the house and make sure your family has enough money to maintain their lifestyle. Losing a loved one is hard enough already.

"So why do we need life insurance as retirees?" Sue asked.

"Well, for the same reason," the Guide replied. "You don't want to leave loose ends and large amounts of debts for your spouse and family to cover. You want to make sure your financial situation is under control. In regard to your family, you may not have any children left at home, but you still want to ensure that your spouse is well taken care of, don't you?

"It goes back to what we discussed with President Roosevelt earlier. Taxes and inflation could very well go up and some income would be lost. The only question is how much. That's why life insurance is so important—to *replace* that lost income."

"I agree with that," President Lincoln said, joining in. "You see, I passed away much earlier than I expected I would. As my assassination proves, there's no telling when or how you will depart this life, and it's best to be prepared."

The Five Crossroads

They watched as the third cornerstone materialized in the corner of the house, making the foundation more solid.

"You've made so much progress," President Lincoln said. He strode back over to his steam-powered wagon. "I have other matters to attend to but I wish you both the best of luck."

"Thank you so much for your help," John said. He shook President Lincoln's hand.

"My pleasure," he added as he adjusted his legs around the steering wheel. He started the contraption and set out down the suburban street, looking rather picturesque. They watched as Lincoln disappeared in the distance.

"Alright," John said, turning his attention back to the Guide, "what's the fourth cornerstone?"

"Well, the fourth cornerstone represents health risks. Up until the age of 65, you most likely have health insurance. Once you turn 65, you trade in your health insurance for Medicare, and many people also purchase Medicare supplements to offset what Medicare won't cover for you."

"I see," John said.

"Your preparations shouldn't stop just at your basic health needs, though," the Guide continued. "There are so many risks to your health as you get older. In addition to daily risks and basic health needs, there are the risks of becoming disabled, and possibly, needing long-term care."

"Is that really very likely?" Sue asked.

"It's much more likely than you think," the Guide replied. "You see, President Lincoln talked to you about the importance of protecting your home and car with proper coverage.

"In 2010, the National Academy of Elder Law Attorneys discovered that the chance of a house fire or car accident being financially devastating to your assets is less than 1%. However, when they measured that same risk with regards to long-term care, they found that it was 50%. That means half of the number of people who need long-term care are financially devastated because of it. That number is going up every year.

"Another factor in your long-term care likeliness is your age. For instance, almost 50% of the Americans over age 65 need long-term care. That number jumps up to 56% after age 85.

"Wow, I didn't realize how much risk we were taking by not considering long-term care," John said.

"That's right," the Guide said. "Long-term care is one of the biggest drains on retirement accounts. It could even cause them to dwindle down to almost nothing."

"That all actually makes sense," John said as he watched the fourth cornerstone appear in the final corner of the financial house. "Now our foundation is complete."

"We're still not completely finished," the Guide said. "The cornerstones are in place but the foundation is not quite done yet."

"What's left?" Sue asked.

The Guide smiled mischievously. "You'll see."

The Five Crossroads

Questions to Consider for Your Retirement

1. Are you building a retirement plan that is unique and specifically tailored to your individual needs?
2. Are you prepared to properly build the four cornerstones of your financial house?
   - Cornerstone 1: Savings
   - Cornerstone 2: Home & Auto Protection
   - Cornerstone 3: Healthcare, Medicare & Long-Term Care
   - Cornerstone 4: Life Insurance/Income Replacement
3. Do you have at least three to twelve months of income put away in savings?
4. Do you have proper coverage on your home(s) and car(s)?
5. Are you aware of the likelihood that you'll need long-term care at least once in your life?
6. Is it important for you to have proper life insurance coverage in your retirement?

Notes

Chapter VI
"The Financial House"

John and Sue stood back to survey their progress on the house thus far. Four cornerstones stood awaiting a foundation that had not yet materialized.

"How do we build the rest of the house?" John asked, excited to continue.

"I'm glad you ask," the Guide replied. "The foundation, walls and roof all represent different types of accounts in which you have invested."

"Our investments?" John asked.

"Why, of course," the Guide answered. "Before we cement in your foundation, allow me to explain the different phases of investments: Accumulation, Preservation and Distribution.

"When you're young and have so much earning time ahead of you, you're in the Accumulation phase. This is the time, if you decide to do so, when you can afford to take more risk in order to try to earn a higher return. At a young age, even if you lose some of the money from your investments, you can still use dollar-cost averaging to your advantage to sometimes come out ahead. You see, you're willing to take more risk because you have more time to make up for losses."

"How long does that phase last?" John asked.

"This phase begins the moment you enter the workforce," the Guide replied, "and lasts until you're about fifty years old or, rather, an age that compels you to think about your retirement more seriously."

John shifted his weight to the other foot while contemplated his own advancing years.

"That's when you enter the Preservation phase. Those in this phase begin to look at their investments a little differently. You start moving the majority of your assets to low-risk, low-volatility and safe, secure accounts. The important difference is that as every year passes, you focus more on *preserving* your money rather than *accumulating* your money. That's why we call this the Preservation phase."

"So, that's the phase we're in?" Sue asked.

"Well, yes, but there's more to it than that," the Guide replied. "You see, you never actually leave the Preservation phase. Your investments should remain in this phase until the day you pass away. However, when you retire, you add the Distribution phase. John, being retired, you've already entered this third phase."

"What's the Distribution phase?" John asked.

"Well, this is the phase of your life when all of your years of saving pay off," the Guide said. "After all, you *were* saving for your retirement, right?"

"That's right," John said, thoughtfully.

"Well, let's talk about your investments and how important it is to work with a retirement guide." He motioned to the blueprints laid out on the nearby workbench. John and Sue moved closer to get a better look.

"First, let's discuss the blueprint of your house," the Guide began. "You see, when you build a house, you want to work closely with an architect who knows your vision, who knows what you aim to create. When you build a financial house, you work with a guide, or a financial architect, who knows what you want out of your retirement and knows how best to make that happen."

"Someone who understands our goals," Sue chimed in.

The Five Crossroads

"That's right," the Guide affirmed. "Based upon those goals, you and your Guide can develop the perfect blueprint for your financial house. Of course, the most important thing to do is focus primarily on your foundation.

"Famous investor Warren Buffet once used these words to describe the ideal investing strategy: 'Rule number one—never lose money. Rule number two—never forget rule number one.' This strategy especially applies to retirees because they don't have time to make up their losses."

"That makes sense," John added.

"So why do we focus on the foundation first?" the Guide asked, rhetorically. "Imagine a tornado or a hurricane tearing through a city. Though these storms are able to tear a house asunder, from an overhead view, you may notice that the foundations of these demolished houses remain."

"Okay," Sue said, "but how does that apply to our finances?"

"I'm glad you ask," the Guide replied. "Changes in the economy can act like a natural disaster when it comes to your financial house. For example, if the market crashed or you experienced a loss of any kind, your house would collapse. In fact, we saw many financial houses destroyed by such a collapse in 2008. Many people lost up to forty percent of their portfolios. Imagine what that can do to your lifestyle."

"We lost quite a bit ourselves and we still haven't fully recovered," John said. "Our advisor kept telling us to hold on."

"I'm sorry to hear that," the Guide said. "It's unfortunate that so many advisors fall back on that strategy."

"Well, howdy folks," a voice with a distinct country drawl suddenly called from behind them. They turned to see a man in a suit and a cowboy hat approaching. "I hope y'all don't mind but Mr. Guide here asked me to come speak to ya."

"John, Sue," the Guide said, motioning toward the man, "I'd like to introduce Will Rogers."

"You mean the actor?" Sue asked, curiously, a little star-struck. The man tipped his hat politely in response.

"That's me, ma'am," Will said. "Mr. Guide asked me to visit with you nice folks in order to tell y'all about the foundation and walls of this here financial house. I s'pose he asked me here 'cause I once said a little somethin' 'bout it."

"What?" John asked curiously.

"I said: 'I am more concerned with the return *of* my money than the return *on* my money.' You see, I was alive during the Depression and at least seven million folks was out of work. Our problem was that there weren't no jobs available for every man who was willin' to work. Let me show you somethin'."

Will Rogers escorted them down the street to a section they hadn't noticed. This part of the street was lined with empty lots and just a few small houses made from fabric sheets drape over structures of poles. The fabric of these houses had doors, windows, and flower pots drawn onto them in chalk. As they gazed at the simple structures, Will Rogers cut in. "This represents the era my financial house was built in. Like yer Guide explained, most of them have their cornerstones and a basic house structure, but the Depression just didn't offer the funds ter build walls and roofs.

"You see, we was one of the richest countries in the world, but we had people starvin' in the streets with no shelter at all. I used to joke that we was the only nation in the history of the world where folks would go to the poor house in an automobile."

They all laughed.

The Five Crossroads

"Truth is, I always tried to use humor to lighten any situation but there weren't nothin' funny about people losing money in the Depression. That's when I decided that I was more concerned with keeping the money I'd earned than I was with making more. Golly, I felt lucky to be earnin' in a time like that anyhow.

"I see," John said. The group turned back and moseyed along to John and Sue's financial plot. "I'm just so grateful to know we're still in a position to build a more solid basis," he added.

"That's where you folks have a great advantage. You have the tools and the means ter build the rest of your financial house. That's why safe, secure accounts and low risk investments are important next," Will said. "When building your financial house with Mr. Guide here, you don't have to worry much about losses. Ask anyone, and they'll tell you that ya can't build a house from the top down. You gotta start at the bottom and work your way up."

"How do you mean?" John asked.

"It means that if you build a solid foundation and sturdy walls in your financial house, you won't have to worry about losing your lifestyle. Don't matter which way the market winds blow or what economic storms appear. Either way, you'll still be standin'."

The Guide nodded his agreement.

"So what is our foundation?" John asked.

"Yer foundation is made up of your investments outside of the market," Will replied. "These accounts have virtually no risk associated with 'em."

"That's why we call them safe, secure accounts in place to keep you from going backward."

"So we should have all our money in those types of accounts?" Sue asked.

"Well, no. Unfortunately with safe, secure accounts, the catch is that the interest isn't as high as the accounts with a little more risk involved. Generally, you'll see an average of three to five percent return over a ten-year period. However, these accounts still play a crucial role in constructing your financial house."

"Why?" John asked.

"Well, you see," the Guide began, "the purpose of investing in these safe, secure accounts is to build a solid foundation within the cornerstones you've already established. This foundation protects your retirement lifestyle. Despite the fluctuation in the market or the economy, this foundation is the strength, or backbone, of all your investments. It's designed to be there for you throughout your retirement."

"Y'all see that house a ways down the street?" Will asked, pointing to a curious structure. The house in question looked worn down and very peculiar. It had a small foundation with walls slanting outward in order to support what appeared to be an enormous roof, reminiscent of a structure in Alice in Wonderland. In fact, the structure looked as if it could collapse under the pressure of the roof alone.

"A storm could take down this house in seconds. The folks that built their financial house that-a-way may see a little more return in the short-term, but if the market ever heads south, and believe me, it could, this house would fall, and they'd have to start over again with whatever foundation they have. And as y'all can see, it ain't much."

"I see," Sue considered, thinking aloud. "So it's important to set aside enough of our funds in our 'foundation' accounts so that, if the market fluctuates, we would still have enough to maintain our lifestyle."

"That's right," the Guide answered.

John nodded his understanding. The couple watched as the foundation materialized, bringing them one step closer to the completion of their financial house.

"What about the walls of our financial house?" John asked.

"Well, do you remember when President Roosevelt mentioned the 3-legged stool?" the Guide asked.

John and Sue nodded.

"This is where that principle comes into play," the Guide said. "While your foundation is there to ensure you can maintain your current lifestyle, your walls are there to keep pace with inflation. Your retirement success depends on working closely with the right Guide and his team to build these walls correctly."

"Team?" Sue asked.

"That's right," the Guide said. "When building a house, you work with an architect to help you with the design. Well, that's the Guide. Your team of wealth money managers represents the contractors. This is the group of experts that oversees the management of your investments. The ideal team works closely with your Guide in order to help build your financial house most efficiently."

"Okay," Sue said. "So this team of wealth money managers is there to make sure we make more money?"

"Well, it ain't quite a promise," Will cut in, "but, you see, a good strategy in the market is about more'n just makin' the most money.

"You see, if you choose ter work with the right architect, or retirement guide, you'll see evidence that they've done their research. The right retirement guide searches 'round the world looking for the right wealth money management team. You see, there are literally thousands of them money managers out there and it requires some work on your guide's part to find the right group to fit yer investment needs. A good retirement guide spends hours 'n hours searching for the right team."

"The right team?" John asked.

"Well," Will said, "what I mean by 'right team' is a group of wealth money managers who's looking out for your best interests. You want to work with a wealth money manager team that's defensive during poor economic times and opportunistic during good economic times. That-a-way, when the market does go down, if you see any losses at all, they'll be much fewer than the average investor's losses. When the market starts on its way up ag'in, while that same average investor will be makin' up losses, you should be seeing gains on your investments."

"That's right," the Guide said. "Your wealth money manager team's primary goal, of course, is to minimize losses in a downward market and increase gains in an upward market. Now, they can't say you won't lose *anything*. Predicting the flow of the market and economy isn't a perfect science yet. Otherwise we'd all know exactly what moves to make next, right?"

"Okay," John said, "so that explains how important it is to work with a qualified team, but what are the walls?"

"The walls represent low-risk, low-volatility investments," the Guide said.

"Low-risk investments sure are important," Will added. "Once y'all have a solid foundation like we talked 'bout, you want to start planning fer the future. Y'all know that safe, secure accounts are there to protect the lifestyle y'all are living right now. But what's going to happen when inflation comes on the scene? Now, it may not happen right off the bat, but yer lifestyle would gradually be chipped away. That's why you got to be investing in low risk accounts. In your time, you might see an average of seven to eight percent return over a ten year period on these types of ac-

The Five Crossroads

counts with much less risk of loss than what y'all would see in high-risk accounts."

"I think I understand," John said.

The four of them watched as the walls suddenly solidified into place, leaving only the roof missing from the nearly completed financial house.

"Once you, yer Guide and his team of wealth money managers have helped raise up your walls, it's time to start lookin' at how to earn a higher return on some of your investments using money that you're willing to use at a higher risk."

"Thanks Mr. Rogers," the Guide said. Turning back to John and Sue, he explained, "now that you have a solid foundation and steady walls, it's time to build your roof. The roof represents high-risk, high-volatility accounts."

"High-risk?" Sue asked. "I thought we shouldn't dabble in high-risk accounts. Isn't that how people get into financial troubles in the first place?"

"A lot of people have that same all-or-nothing mentality," the Guide replied. "They put everything they have in high-risk accounts only to lose money, panic and pull everything out. What do they do with it then? They invest it in a savings account or, worse, hide it under their mattress. Take a look at the house right across the street, for example." The house he motioned to had tall walls that slanted inward, nearly to a point. The roof they did have was very small and barely covered the top of the house.

"Those folks were scared off by the 'risk factor.' True, they've significantly reduced their chances of losing money with those types of investments, but they're also not getting the higher return that the higher-risk investments potentially offer."

Sue nodded in understanding.

"The truth is, no, you don't want all your money to sit in stocks and mutual funds that have a higher potential for loss," the Guide continued. "But high-risk investments do sometimes have a place in your financial portfolio once you've built your foundation and walls. That way, should you lose anything from the accounts that make up your roof, you can still live comfortably on the money invested in your foundation and walls."

"So, we shouldn't invest a lot of money in high-risk accounts until we've built our four cornerstones, a steady foundation and solid walls?" John asked.

"That's right," the Guide answered. "If your guide is working with the right wealth money managers, though, you'll be taking fewer risks even within your high-risk investments. These wealth money managers have worked with investments for years and have used their experience to put together a model, or a system of tactical management, that helps reduce your risk."

"I think that was our biggest problem," John said, "putting too much of our money in the rooftop of our finances without the walls and foundation to support it. It seems like we need to take a closer look at how we build our financial house. But how much should we put into our foundation and walls before we invest in the roof?"

"Well, remember that everyone's situation is different," the Guide said, "but there is a simple rule to keep in mind when you look at your portfolio. This rule can help you protect the money you already have while still capitalizing on your chance to grow."

"There's a rule?" Sue asked.

"Yes," the Guide replied, "and it's called the Rule of One Hundred."

"How does it work?" Sue ventured.

The Five Crossroads

"Well, the Rule of One Hundred states that if you take one hundred percent of your assets and subtract the percentage equal to your age, you should have no more than what remains invested in high-risk, high volatility accounts. For example, if you are age 65, you should have no more than 35% of your money in high risk investments. The other 65% should be invested in safe, secure and low-risk, low-volatility investments."

"That *is* simple," John said.

"Also, the Rule of One Hundred is just a basic guideline. In reality, you should work closely with a retirement guide, who shares your vision for your financial house. The percentage you invest in each part of your house should be based upon your comfort level."

John and Sue watched as the roof appeared, completing their financial house. With John's cue, they gratefully removed their hard hats.

"John, Sue, you've done a wonderful job building your financial house, especially with risk management in mind, but there are still so many things I have to share with you," the Guide said.

"Lead on," John said, confidently. "Thank you, Mr. Rogers, for your time. We appreciate it, and it was an absolute privilege to meet you."

"Aw shucks. It was nice to meet y'all, too," Will said, reaching forward and shaking both their hands. "Y'all take care now." With that he sauntered off down the road, whistling a tune.

As the Smiths walked further down the sidewalk, the neighborhood disappeared behind them into the air and the Smiths once again found themselves traveling on a dirt path, beckoning them forward toward the adventure ahead.

Questions to Consider for Your etirement

1. Do you understand the three different phases of your investments? What phase are you in? Do your investment choices reflect that phase?
   - Accumulation
   - Preservation
   - Distribution
2. How have your goals changed throughout your life? How has your retirement portfolio been affected by those changes?
3. Are you more concerned with the return *on* your money or the return *of* your money?
4. Do you have a solid foundation of safe, secure accounts to help you maintain your current lifestyle, regardless of the fluctuation of the market and the economy?
5. Are your low-risk, low-volatility investments helping you keep pace with inflation?
6. Are you working with a team of highly qualified professionals?
7. Are your retirement investments being managed by wealth money managers who are opportunistic in good times and defensive in bad times?
8. Have you taken the time to prepare your own financial blueprint?

Notes

Chapter VII
"Staying Afloat"

As they traveled the path ahead, John and Sue felt a wave of relief wash over them. They felt that if they continued their journey with the Guide, their retirement years would be much more enjoyable than they had previously hoped.

The Guide soon led them to another crossroad. The terrain and the weather transformed, and the Smiths felt a humid air stirring in the wind. The path beneath their feet softened with a touch of moisture, and the trees were lush, boasting several different hues of green. They approached a worn, plank dock jutting out over a vast, slow-moving river enclosed by dense trees on either end. Intuitively, they felt they were looking at the mighty Mississippi. A riverboat gently putted up to the dock and came to a stop.

"It looks like we're just in time," the Guide said. "Come on, follow me."

John and Sue followed the Guide onto the dock. Beside the ramp that led up to the boat, there was a man in a wicker chair. He wore a brilliant white suit that matched the color of his hair and his thick mustache, and he smoked a pipe as he watched them approach.

"Welcome," the man said, standing and shaking the Guide's hand. "It's been a while."

"Yes it has," the Guide replied. "I've brought along a few friends of mine. I hope you don't mind. Allow me to introduce you to John and Sue Smith."

"I most certainly don't mind," the man replied. "John, Sue, it's wonderful to meet you. My name is Samuel Clemens. Most people call me by my pen name, however, Mark Twain. Either is fine by me."

"Mark Twain," Sue repeated, "as in *The Adventures of Huckleberry Finn*?"

"Yes ma'am," Mr. Twain said, nodding proudly.

"That's incredible," Sue said. "I've read nearly everything you've ever published."

"Have you?" Mark asked, smiling. "I always love meeting a fan." The boat let out a deep whistle and a puff of smoke impatiently. Mark Twain looked up as if suddenly remembering the boat was there. "Oh yes, shall we?" he asked, offering his hand to Sue and helping her up the ramp onto the deck of the riverboat.

"You're in safe hands ma'am. I'm sure many people in your time know me as a writer," Mr. Twain said, "but not too many know that I was also a riverboat pilot."

"I didn't," Sue said, impressed.

"Well, allow me to show you," Mark replied. "Would you fancy a ride down the river as we chat?"

"I would love that," Sue replied. "Is that the Mississippi?"

"It certainly is," Mr. Twain said. "But it's not just the Mississippi; this here is also the juncture of the **Debt Elimination Crossroad**."

"Debt?" Sue asked.

"That's right. I'm here to talk to you about the importance of paying off your debts."

"Mr. Twain, it's amazing to meet you, sir," John said, "but I am a little curious as to what a writer or a riverboat pilot could teach us about retirement?"

"Well, I'm an expert on the Debt Elimination Crossroad," Twain chuckled. "I became an expert of debt elimi-

The Five Crossroads

nation because of the mistakes I made and the lessons I was forced to learn in the process," Twain replied with characteristic candor.

"Like what?" John asked.

Mark Twain moved to the helm of the ship and guided the boat out into the open, clear waters of the Mississippi. "Well, you see, I made quite a bit of money from my books and other writings," Twain began, "but I also made some poor investment choices. The main blow came when I invested many of my funds in a new typesetting device that failed miserably. With my newest book gathering only scant success coupled with my mismanagement of the funds, I was left in financial ruin.

"Wanting to protect everything I'd worked so hard for," Twain said, "I filed for bankruptcy and transferred the copyrights of all my works to my wife, Olivia. I was determined to work my way back out of financial ruin."

I traveled the world in 1895, delivering lecture after lecture to raise enough money to pay off what remained of my debts after the bankruptcy. I had a handle on my debt after one year and had raised enough money to be debt-free by 1900."

"You paid off all your debts in five years?" John asked.

"I did," he answered somewhat smugly, steering the boat through a wide river bend. "You see, having the debt hanging above my head caused me a lot of stress. It created health problems, and it put a strain on my marriage. In fact, one of the main causes of divorce both in my time and in yours is financial trouble. Debt is the premier financial problem in America."

"That's why we recommend putting together a plan-of-action to pay off any debts you may have," the Guide added. "You see, the first step in paying off your debts is making the commitment to do so. After that, it's actually pretty simple."

"We've been paying off debts for years," John said with a sigh. "It can't be that simple."

"Well, after you've made the commitment to see it done, it's as simple as knowing where you've been. John, you said you've been paying off debts for years. That means you already have the desire. I'm assuming your goal is to pay off all your debts."

"Yes it is," John said resolutely.

"Of course it is," the Guide said. "We all know interest is better to earn than to pay. As Mr. Twain said, debt can create a lot of stress. Stress can cause health problems and it can put pressure on not only your marriage, but your family relationships as well. How do we fix that? We solve our debt problem with budgeting."

"Budgeting?" Sue asked.

"Yes, you can't know where you're going until you know where you've been. In other words, you have to understand where every cent you spend is going. How can you keep track of every cent? It's simple. I recommend carrying a notebook with you everywhere you go, every day for thirty days. Every time you make a purchase, even if it's a five cent candy, scratch it in on your notebook."

"This is something Olivia and I did," Mark Twain added from the helm. "We took note of everything we did with our money. Soon, we were able to see where we were spending money unnecessarily. We went through each one of our expenses and decided how much money we needed to cover our bases.

"After you do that, it's best to split everything else evenly between saving and paying off your debts. Pay the minimum amount for each debt, like the minimum due on a credit card, and then use the rest of your debt budget toward the smallest debt. Once your smallest debt is entirely paid, apply a quarter of the money you were paying toward

The Five Crossroads

that debt to savings. You use the rest toward the next smallest debt. That way, you can just continue up the ladder from smallest to largest until all your debts are paid off."

"You pay off the smallest debt first?" John asked.

"Of course," the Guide answered. "Would you rather be paying multiple creditors or just one? The amount isn't important. The fewer creditors you have to pay, the less stressful paying off debts will be."

"What about spending money?" Sue asked.

"Well, if you must have some open spending funds," Mr. Twain answered, "I suggest budgeting out as little as possible and never spending above that amount."

"That's wonderful in theory," John said, "but even though I'm a saver, I'll admit that I spend a few dollars here and there without batting an eye. How do you keep insignificant spending under control?"

The Guide considered the question. "First, you need to determine if your purchase is something you *want*, or something you *need*. Repairing the transmission in your car is something on which you *need* to spend your money. Buying a big screen TV, on the other hand, is only something you *want*. You could live just as well without it.

"Next, I suggest promising yourself a 24-hour pondering time," the Guide continued. "Any time you feel you *need* something, leave your credit card behind when you shop around and when you believe you've found what you want, go home and sleep on it. If, after a 24-hour period, you still feel that you can't do without it, go back and purchase it. If you find that it isn't necessary for your life to continue in comfort, don't purchase it."

"What about small purchases like eating out?" Sue asked.

"Well, I suggest putting together an envelope budgeting program," the Guide said.

"Envelope budgeting?" Sue asked. "How does that work?"

"Well, you designate an envelope for each of your expenses and when you're paid, you put the budgeted amount into the envelope in cash. Once the cash runs out, you're no longer allowed to spend in that category."

John and Sue listened curiously as the riverboat chugged along. The sun was sinking ever so slowly into the tree-line as the day slipped by like their boat through the river.

"For instance, you mentioned eating out. If you designate 100 dollars a month toward eating out, and you go out to a fancy restaurant and spend that 100 all in one night, you don't go out to eat for the rest of the month. The envelope method was created long ago, but now-a-days, you can find budgeting apps that can help you create a budgeting plan right on your phone, tablet, or computer. They tell you how much you're allowed to spend in a certain area like eating out, entertainment or other categories."

"Another good tip when it comes to dining out is sharing," Mark Twain added. "When Olivia and I would spend a night out on the town, we would share a meal and order an extra salad. Almost every restaurant makes a meal big enough to have your fill and then some. Order waters instead of soda. After a few months, you'll likely see a thicker wallet and a thinner waistline," Twain joked.

"Those are excellent ideas," John said, chuckling. "I wonder why we never considered it before."

The riverboat turned and they could see a nearby dock ahead. A beautiful restaurant sat on the dock, lit up by lanterns and candles against the shadowy hues of the golden sunset slanting through the trees.

The Five Crossroads

"I'm going to let the two of you enjoy a wonderful dinner together," the Guide said, "but perhaps your conversation should linger on some new debt elimination strategies.

"Also, remember this. We talked a short time ago about the importance of a solid foundation. Make sure that you have the three to twelve months salary safely nestled in savings before you truly begin focusing on debt elimination. Why? Because that's exactly what your savings is for—to prevent debt in the future."

"And now, I'm afraid this is your stop," Mark Twain said, expertly gliding the riverboat against the wooden dock. "John, Sue, I can see that you've learned so much on your journey, but there is still quite an adventure ahead of you. Enjoy your dinner, and I hope to see you both again sometime soon."

"You too," John said, shaking Mark Twain's hand. Then he turned and winked at Sue. "Dinner smells wonderful, and I bet there's a nice plate with our name on it."

Mr. Twain laughed as he helped them onto the dock and returned to the helm.

"Farewell," he shouted as he turned the boat back upstream. John and Sue waved until the riverboat was out of sight.

"Well," the Guide said, "I'll leave you two alone. I hope you enjoy dinner, and I'll be waiting right here when you're finished."

"Thank you," John said, sincerely.

Questions to Consider for Your Retirement

1. Did you know that one of the most important aspects of paying off debts is simply having the desire to do so? Do you have the desire to pay off your debts?
2. Have you taken the time to prepare a budget?
3. Do you know where every cent you spend is going?
4. When shopping, do you take the time to make a distinction between *want* and *need*? Do you give yourself 24 hours to consider your bigger purchases?
5. What sacrifices have you made in order to pay off your debts? How much more could you afford to sacrifice?

Notes

Chapter VIII
"Leaving a Legacy"

When they had finished their elegant dinner, John and Sue stood and surveyed the dock where they'd landed. After locating their Guide on a nearby dirt path, they headed toward him.

As they approached, they could see he was lost in thought, staring down the path that lay ahead of them.

The Guide roused himself as he noticed the Smiths approaching. He smiled kindly at them and motioned toward the path.

"Shall we?" he asked.

"You look more serious than usual," John pried.

"I was hoping we could beat this storm," the Guide said, "but it looks like we're going to have to travel through it." The Guide pointed toward the sky in the distance. A wave of rolling grey clouds closed in on the path ahead covering the last streams of light from the setting sun.

The Smiths stared up at the grey sky ahead of them, hearing the heavy sound of thunder in the distance. Sue suddenly squinted and leaned forward, trying to make something out. There was some sort of colorful object blowing around wildly within the clouds.

"What is that?" she asked, speaking more to herself than to anyone else. She pointed at the object and both John and the Guide looked into the distance.

"Oh," the Guide said understandingly, "so that's why the storm is rolling in."

"What do you mean?" John asked.

"That little red object thrashing about in the wind," the Guide said, pointing to it and then tracing his finger downward to the path, "is a kite." Ahead, they saw a somewhat portly gentleman with a balding head rimmed by a shock of long, white hair frantically guiding his kite this way and that through the tumultuous wind. A bolt of lightning streaked across the sky, dangerously close to the little kite.

"Is he crazy?" Sue shouted as they moved down the dirt road. "Why would he be flying a kite in this weather?"

"Ah, well, he's done it before," the Guide said with a wink. "He's another close friend of mine."

"Who is he?" John asked, curiously.

"He's an inventor of sorts and is responsible for early designs of some of the things you use every day," the Guide said as they came closer to the man.

When they approached him, he waved at them wildly, still clinging tightly to the kite string.

"John, Sue, allow me to introduce you to Benjamin Franklin," the Guide said as they stopped in the path to greet one another.

"Well, hello," Mr. Franklin said, smiling. He shook their hands cordially while he still held tightly to the kite string. "It's wonderful to meet you both. If you'll follow me we can talk somewhere a little more comfortable and a little less stormy. I'll catch more lightning one of these days."

He expertly reeled in his kite and tucked it under his arm as he escorted them back to his cabin, welcomed them inside and closed the door. Inside, a fire crackled warmly, and they were glad to be out of the grasp of the elements.

"That's better," he said. "We can't have you face your last crossroad in that sort of weather. A nice warm home is a much better setting, don't you agree?"

The Five Crossroads

"Why, thank you," Sue said, smoothing out her wind-blown hair. "We've learned so much today. We're looking forward to learning about the fifth crossroad, especially from one of the founding fathers."

"Well, let's get right to it then, shall we? This is the **Legacy Planning** Crossroad," Benjamin Franklin replied. "Let me begin with a question. How are you planning to pass on your legacy?"

"When we pass away, our money will be given to our children," John answered.

"That's interesting," Franklin said, stoking the fire a bit. "Were you aware that over half the children who receive an inheritance spend seventy percent of it within the first ninety days?"

"Our children are more responsible than that," Sue said candidly.

"Some children are very responsible but some aren't," Franklin said. "Perhaps they wanted a bigger home or a nicer car. There's nothing irresponsible about improving life's comforts, but would you really want your life savings going into one source all at once? Here's your basic rule of thumb to follow: ask yourselves, if you were still alive, would you be willing to give your children the money to spend on these new assets?"

John and Sue thought for a moment. "It would be nice to have that sort of control, but we won't exactly be around to enforce it. How do we prevent them from doing so?" John asked.

"What if I told you there was a way to control how much money they could use at any one given time?" Franklin asked. "Additionally, what if you could also spread the tax responsibility over many years, even throughout several generations? In fact, in the long run, you could end up leaving your heirs ten times the amount that you originally planned to leave to them."

"It sounds complicated," John answered. "Is this program something new?"

"Not at all," Mr. Franklin answered. "In fact, I was able to use a similar program in my time. Did you know that I left behind a meager £2,000 at the time of my death? This money was given evenly to the good people of Boston and Philadelphia. That was worth about $4,400 in my day; in your time it would be worth closer to about $55,000. It doesn't sound like much, but I asked that it not be presented to either city until 1990. By that time, the account I left to Boston had grown to over $2,000,000. Philadelphia's account grew even larger to almost $5,000,000. Though I passed away in 1788, my legacy is still providing money for those dear places I cherished in my lifetime."

"That's over two hundred years," John said in amazement, "but Sue and I wanted our money to be paid out right after we pass away. We don't care to wait as long as you did."

"Well, that's fine," Franklin said. "You can choose to defer it to be distributed at any date you wish, or you can even design the payments to be distributed immediately in one bulk sum, or over the course of a specified length of time.

"That's not all legacy planning entails, though. In order to set up my estate properly, I needed to work with an attorney. You see, any retirement guide worth your time will work with a highly qualified team of professionals. You already learned about the wealth money managers, right?"

"Yes, we did," Sue replied, intrigued.

"Well, another important part of that team of professionals is an attorney," Franklin replied. "You see, working with many different financial professionals is similar

The Five Crossroads

to working with health professionals. I'm sure you've both been to a doctor at least once, right?"

"A few more times than that, Mr. Franklin," John said, chuckling.

"Then you'll know exactly what I'm talking about," he replied. "No matter how many times you fill out that darn paperwork, every time you see a new doctor or some kind of medical specialist, you have to fill out the forms again."

"That's true," John said.

"Well, the same thing applies to financial professionals. It's much simpler to work with a financial team who communicates regularly about your situation. That way, you can avoid explaining yourself to advisors and attorneys time and time again."

"That would be nice," Sue said.

"That's why it's important that you work with a guide supported by a team of professionals, one of whom should be an estate attorney," Mr. Franklin said. "That way, you can work out all the legal requirements for planning your estate as you wish. You can find the best way to avoid paying the estate tax like my friend Roosevelt explained.

"An attorney can help align and scrutinize all of the details that you could miss on your own. An attorney sets up all the documents you need. He sets up trusts that avoid probate and that also set certain guidelines for whatever assets your beneficiaries inherit and how they will be distributed. He helps you create wills to determine which beneficiaries receive which assets or property upon your passing. An attorney can also help you name someone to make legal, medical and financial decisions for you should you become unable to do so."

"I think it's great that retirement guides choose to work with attorneys," John said, "but what if we choose to work with a personal friend of ours? He's an amazing defense attorney and we feel really comfortable with him."

"Well, it's usually best to work with someone who makes you feel comfortable, but not necessarily in this case. If your friend were an estate attorney, I'd say go right ahead, but a defense, criminal law, or a divorce attorney won't have the specialty training or expertise required to set your estate up properly. It's like going to a foot doctor to treat your trouble with migraines. If you have a friend or family member who is an estate attorney, by all means, you ought to work with them. However, any other type of attorney most likely won't be qualified to give you advice on your estate."

"Okay," John said, a little disappointed. "I guess that makes sense. That could lead to some pretty big mistakes that we wouldn't want to risk."

"It certainly can," Franklin agreed. "One of the biggest mistakes that we've seen in our own personal experience together is how beneficiary designations are set up."

"What do you mean?" Sue asked.

"Well, a lot of people don't put too much thought into their beneficiary designations. It seems like an easy blank to fill in, right? However, a lot of people don't take this one thing into account—life. Life happens. The Guide and I have seen that many people we've chosen to work with don't have their beneficiaries set up properly. Their designations often contain minor oversights that can cause major stress and confusion when you're no longer there to explain the matter."

"What kind of oversights?" John queried.

"Major life changes, for instance. If you get married, it's probably time to take mom and dad off your beneficiary designation and add your spouse. When you have children, you may want to add them. If you get divorced, odds are you don't want all your money given to your ex in the end,

The Five Crossroads

especially if you get remarried. That kind of mistake can cause a lot of hurt and angry feelings over an unintentional mistake."

Outside, a heavy rain descended, pattering on the roof and windows. The sky was dark except for the bright flashes of lightning now and then.

"All of our accounts are updated properly," John said. "We designated one another as our beneficiary should we pass away."

"That's wonderful," Franklin said. "Who else is on your beneficiary designations?"

"Well, no one," Sue answered. "After all, whichever spouse survives the other will leave whatever they have left to the children when they die as well."

"That sounds like a good plan except for one thing you may not have taken into account," Ben Franklin said solemnly. "What happens if you both were to die in a car accident tomorrow? We hope it won't happen but we've seen that circumstance before. What happens to your estate then?"

"Well, I suppose our children would get it," John answered.

"And they very well may," Mr. Franklin replied, "after several months, perhaps even years, in court battles over who deserves what."

"Our children aren't greedy," Sue said confidently. "They'd work it out in the end."

"I wouldn't be so sure," Franklin said. "It's not that I believe your children are self-serving, but every child may feel entitled to something. For instance, do you have a particular child who lives closer than the others and visits more often?"

"Yes," Sue answered. "Our daughter often invites us to dinner and brings her children to visit. We love those times and we'd like to leave something special behind for her."

"How wonderful," Benjamin Franklin said. "Now, though these visits don't mean that you love her any more than your other children, as you mentioned, you may want to do something extra special for one of your children. That's one of the many reasons why legacy planning is important. You can leave behind a specific heirloom to your daughter if you'd like."

"Good," John said.

"That's why, under the primary beneficiary—in this case, your spouse—you want to add contingent beneficiaries. You can choose to add your children, your grandchildren, or even a charity. In fact, you can add all three if you prefer and it can be split evenly among them or broken down differently as you see fit."

"That's something we'll have to look at," John said, turning to Sue. "I thought we were all taken care of in that department."

"Unfortunately, many people do," Franklin said. "Another thing to think about is the rule of *Per Stirpes*."

"What is that?" John asked.

"Well, heaven forbid, but what if one of your children passes away before you do?" Franklin asked. "Would you want their share of the money to be split between his or her siblings or passed down to his or her children instead? It's something to think about if you have grandchildren."

"Wow," Sue exclaimed. "I never realized how much thought goes into such a seemingly simple document."

"It's a simple document, you're right," the Guide said, nodding. "However, it's those simple mistakes that cause your beneficiaries a lot of stress, time and money to set things right if it's even possible to do so. In fact, since we've

The Five Crossroads

been talking about children and grandchildren, I know several of my friends have less than perfect relationships with their sons-in-law or daughters-in-law. Many options allow you to control your beneficiary designations and the way in which their distributions are paid out so your money can remain directly in the family if you choose."

"We'll make sure to fix those things as soon as possible," John said. "Thank you for all of this valuable information."

"You're very welcome," Franklin replied. "After deciding on your children's benefits, it's time to think about you for a little while. There's another aspect of legacy planning that just involves you. Don't worry, your children won't mind."

"Think about us? Why would we need legacy planning for ourselves?" Sue asked.

"Another important aspect of legacy planning is planning for your funeral," Benjamin Franklin said. "The right guide can help you plan the entire process of your final farewell. Here's where that team of professionals comes in handy again. Your personal guide should be working closely with a local mortuary to determine all the details, from how the flowers will be funded to who will be speaking at the service."

"Really?" John asked. "They have programs like that?"

"Yes, they do," Franklin replied. "In fact, this step will also benefit your family. Instead of spending time trying to plan out the funeral program, your friends and family can spend more time together. It will give them time to grieve, yes, but it will also give them time to share your stories and the beautiful memories they shared with you, without frustration looming overhead. It would be nice to know that your family could dedicate time and energy to remembering the good times you shared with them."

"I hadn't considered that before," John said. "I hope they have the time to remember me fondly without the stress of a funeral."

"Well, John, Sue, I know I will remember you fondly," Benjamin Franklin said. "It appears you've come to the end of your first journey with the Guide."

"What do you mean?" Sue asked.

"You've done it," Franklin replied. "You've traveled through the five crossroads, and you're ready now to take action. I'll see you both again soon. Farewell and good luck."

With that, Benjamin Franklin tucked his kite under his arm and stepped back out into the blustery weather. John and Sue exchanged wry smiles.

"He's right," the Guide said. "After learning so much, you've completed your journey. Are you ready to go back?"

"I suppose we are," John sighed somewhat sadly. "After all, we have quite a list of goals to accomplish."

"Well, when you're ready to return to the office, simply close your eyes."

"What, we don't need to click any ruby slippers together?" Sue said with a laugh in her voice.

The Guide winked.

Sue took John's hand and squeezed tightly. They silently soaked in the journey they'd completed in just one amazing day. Sue hugged John's arm tightly, and John gently kissed her forehead.

"On three?" John asked.

"On three," Sue agreed.

"One, two," John said, pausing for one last look around at the magical world they'd stumbled upon. "Three."

They closed their eyes.

The Five Crossroads

Questions to Consider for Your Retirement

1. Were you aware that over half the children who are left an inheritance spend 70% within the first 90 days?
2. Have you set up both primary and secondary beneficiaries correctly?
3. Did you know that without proper planning, your beneficiaries could be liable for your tax responsibility?
4. Are you working with a team of highly qualified professionals that work together to keep your retirement plan consistent? Does that team include an estate attorney to assist you with trusts, wills and power of attorney documents?
5. Have you properly set up your beneficiaries in order to see that distributions follow your bloodline per stirpes?
6. Have you taken the time now to make all preparations for the proper handling your funeral and estate after you pass away?

Notes

Chapter IX
"Final Reflections"

When the Smiths opened their eyes, they found themselves once again in the little square room with the painting on the wall. The wind was no longer blowing, but Uncle Sam stood smiling and bowing under the tree.

"Welcome back," the Guide said from behind them. "I trust you enjoyed your journey."

John jumped at the sound of his voice and then chuckled to himself. Turning to face him, he said, "It was beyond what we could have imagined, literally. Thank you so much."

John shook the Guide's hand firmly, scarcely believing that the prior events had really happened.

"Don't thank me just yet," the Guide said. "I still have one more surprise for you before you go."

"Another surprise?" Sue asked in disbelief.

"Yes," the Guide said, smiling mischievously. "A little something to remind you of your journey today."

He walked over to a side door in the opposite corner of the room, and, turning back to John and Sue, recited nearly verbatim the very words he used earlier.

"Now, are you absolutely sure that you're ready to take the next step on your journey toward the perfect retirement?"

John and Sue glanced at one another, feeling like they had gained years of wisdom since morning. They both looked at the Guide eagerly.

"Yes," John said, glowing with a newfound confidence.

The Guide slowly pushed open the door with a creak.

John and Sue's eyes grew wide as they gazed around the room. It was a quiet, unassuming room with the wallpaper peeling just a bit in the corners. The room looked old. A single piece of furniture stood against the far wall: a wardrobe-sized antique mirror, nearly as tall as the room itself. John and Sue approached the mirror to find that it held no reflection at all, but rather an opaque mist that swirled within the large oval of glass. The Smiths looked back questioningly at the Guide for an explanation.

"I hope you don't mind," he said, "but I thought you'd like a chance to say goodbye to all the friends you've made along the way."

"Of course we would," Sue said, her eyes widening with hope. "How…" Her voice trailed off as a figure materialized within the misty haze in the mirror. Suddenly, Uncle Sam stood before them tipping his hat in his friendly manner once more.

"Oh, Uncle Sam!" Sue gasped, delighted.

"Remember, my dear friends," he began with a smile, "the government has provided several opportunities for you to reduce your taxes. Use the analogies about the milk pails to remind you where you ought to store your money. Also, remember that if you defer your taxes, it's like avoiding the tax on the seeds only to pay tax on the crops."

"That's right! We'll try to always move our money toward the tax-free, estate tax-free pail," Sue answered.

Uncle Sam chuckled and nodded. "You've got it." His figure slowly swirled back into the misty background, while another man came into focus. It was John's ancestor whom they met at the Boston Tea Party.

"John, my boy, never forget," Linus T. Smith said, stepping forward, "we live in a wonderful country, but you should always stand up for what is yours. Use the tax laws to your advantage. That's why they're there for you." He gave

The Five Crossroads

John an affectionate wink before he too vanished back into the swirl. John and Sue smiled.

Next from the fog came the spokes of a wheelchair. "And of course you can't forget the legs of the three-legged stool: Social Security, Pensions and, most importantly, Savings and Investments," President Roosevelt said, wheeling himself forward. "Remember, the Savings and Investments leg is the only one you have control over. You've got to take care of your own money. Nobody's going to do it for you."

"Thank you, Mr. President," Sue said, inclining her head down in a soft, appreciative nod. Roosevelt returned the gesture and gave a departing wave as his reflection blurred, his fingertips fading last.

President Lincoln materialized next. He stepped forward and pointed an assertive finger at the couple.

"John and Sue," President Lincoln said, "when you build your financial house, begin by constructing the four cornerstones: Savings, Home and Auto Insurance, Life Insurance, and Health Insurance & Medicare.

"Try to set aside three to twelve months' income put into savings in case of emergencies and protect your home and your modern-day car from losses with proper insurance coverage. Don't forget that life insurance isn't only for the young, but it also serves as valuable protection from the loss of your spouse's income should you pass away.

"Lastly, remember that your health costs will go up during your retirement. You'll need health insurance until you can apply for Medicare. Also, since half of the retirees in America need long-term-care at one point, it's best to be prepared as I'm sure you will be, my dear friends."

"Thank you, sir, we couldn't have built our financial house without you," John said quickly as Lincoln's tall figure wafted away.

Will Roger's cowboy drawl rang out before he even appeared. "It's up to y'all to make sure that yer house keeps on standin' firm." He stood before them, leaning to one side and smiling. "Remember to work with a guide and their team ter help y'all build a solid foundation using them safe, secure accounts. Once yer there, you can focus more on building your walls and roof. Make sure them team members are defensive in bad times and opportunistic in good times."

"Thank you, Will, we'll remember" Sue said, smiling as the mist took him away.

"Stick to a budget," Mark Twain said, stepping forward from the fog. "Remember, in order to know where your money's going, you have to know where it's been. Make a plan to pay off all your debts, and keep at it till it's done. That plan worked for me," he said smugly.

"And don't forget that you don't have to do much to save money. Decide if your purchases are needs or just wants, wait twenty four hours before making a big purchase, and don't be afraid to share a meal and order waters. If you're going to save money and get out of debt, you might as well stay in shape too, right?"

"That's right," John said.

He gave them a hearty laugh as his image faded. Benjamin Franklin cleared his throat as the mist cleared, drawing their attention. He adjusted his vest briefly and looked at them with the warmth of a father.

"Don't forget to work with a qualified team of professionals led by a retirement guide," he said, "and make certain your team has an estate attorney. That way you can be sure you have the right documents. Remember, the different options you have when you set up your legacy. Don't forget to arrange your beneficiaries properly. Work with your Guide and the attorney to make sure that everything will

The Five Crossroads

happen just the way you want. We all wish you the best as you continue on."

"We'll remember everything," John said, reluctant to see him go. "Thank you."

Ben Franklin gave them one last, fading smile as the mist gathered around him. The mist swirled silently in the mirror as the procession ended. John and Sue turned around to their Guide in awe.

"And thank you so much, Guide," Sue said, softly. "Today has been an amazing journey."

"Today," the Guide said, "is not the end of your journey. Take a look in the mirror one last time."

As they looked back at the mirror, the mist cleared completely leaving John and Sue gazing at their own reflections, side by side, ready to step forward.

"Today was only the first few steps of your real adventure. You have the rest of your lives ahead of you. Your journey is far from over. Always remember that taking the first step is the most difficult. If we procrastinate, nothing gets done. By taking this first step, you have made the retirement of your dreams possible."

"Thank you," John said, shaking his hand. "We're looking forward to seeing you again soon."

"As am I," the Guide replied with a final tender smile.

The Smiths stood before the mirror for a moment more. Then they walked hand in hand out the door, the Guide watching them from the open doorway.

There was no need to look back. They were confident that they were set on the right track for a retirement filled with joy and accomplished dreams.

John opened the door for Sue before climbing into the driver's seat. He took the wheel between his hands and looked over at Sue.

"Well," John asked as he started the car and a mischievous smile appeared on his face, "which path should we take?"

The End, or Rather, the Beginning...

Made in the USA
Charleston, SC
09 May 2013